# BEAUTY FOR ASHES

## JACQUELINE FUSALLAH

Copyright © 2019

***BEAUTY FOR ASHES***
By Jacqueline Fusallah

All rights reserved. No part of this book may be used or reproduced by any means, graphic, electronic, or mechanical, including photocopying, recording, taping or by any information storage retrieval system without the written permission of the publisher except in the case of brief quotations embodied in critical articles and reviews. Because of the dynamic nature of the Internet, any web addresses or links contained in this book may have changed since publication and may no longer be valid. The views expressed in this work are solely those of the author and do not necessarily reflect the views of the publisher, and the publisher hereby disclaims any responsibility for them.

ISBN-13: 978-1694164322

All Scripture quotations, unless otherwise indicated, are taken from the: King James Version of the Holy Bible. All Scripture quotations are used by permission. Scripture marked (NKJV) are taken from the New King James Version®. Copyright © 1982 by Thomas Nelson, Inc. Used by permission. Scripture quotations marked (NIV) are taken from the Holy Bible, New International Version®, NIV®. Copyright © 1973, 1978, 1984, 2011 by Biblica, Inc.™ Used by permission of Zondervan. All rights reserved worldwide. www.zondervan.com. The "NIV" and "New International Version" are trademarks registered in the United States Patent and Trademark Office by Biblica, Inc.™

    Editing / Interior Book Design & Layout / Publishing Assistance
                    CBM Christian Book Editing
                  www.christian-book-editing.com

Printed in the United States of America

****

# PREFACE

In my book, *Beauty for Ashes*, I draw the reader's attention to learn what it means to be a child of the everlasting King. Your richest duty is devotion to Jesus Christ your Lord and Savior. It urges the reader to see through the eyes of Scripture God's perspective to man's suffering, the power of God's Word and the transforming power of the Holy Spirit to those who believe.

You are human and you surely suffer. But do you understand your suffering or sin? Do I understand my own? Can suffering be understood by us all? Is it possible to learn, or even be enriched, by pain and trouble? Can we draw nearer to our Creator and Savior through suffering? Jesus indicates that suffering is a kind of "pruning" that will lead to more abundant spiritual fruitfulness. Some people trip and fall upon themselves. Many others absorb kicks, the slings, and the arrows of their fellow man. You already know what it means to be crushed by the many weights of living. Some like Jacob, wrestle mightily and then walk away from their trial with a noticeable, permanent limp. That limp is the outward sign that they have been hurt and are humbled inside. To walk with a limp, whatever its cause, is to be continuously humbled. One is humbled in suffering only if one can see from God's perspective.

A limp is our shared, inherent human weakness and inability to carry the weight of existence alone. In *Beauty for Ashes*, I indicate through Scripture to the reader that Jesus' Presence with them is nearer than they think, even richly present in all their moments. Then I relate how to overcome past and present struggles. All these truths are backed by Scripture, to enlighten, embolden and inspire the reader. The shared limp is a "symptom" constantly reminding us of the distance we have fallen from God. It is a metaphor of our need to be forgiven and sanctified. It becomes a sign of one's understanding of total dependence upon our Lord who is the Star illuminating our path.

These truths drawn from the Bible are lined up in *Beauty for Ashes* to reach the hurting, to lift up those who are bowed down by the pressure of life, and to enlighten those who are blinded by the cares of this world, or those who desire a deeper intimate walk with our Lord Jesus Christ.

All things are not God sent but all things are God used.

At thirteen years-of-age, I was raped by two men. When they released me, I was so scared and helpless. I also felt sick to my stomach...upset and confused, I had no idea where I was. I painfully got up on my feet after the trauma with fear and not a clue which direction home was. I prayed amid my sobbing, I didn't know that part of town. "God please help me to get home..." AND HE DID, His Presence was with me. There are many victims of sexual abuse who suffer silently. Young girls and boys, teenage boys and teenage girls suffer as victims. There are also many adults who endure sexual abuse, and likewise suffer silently at the hands of their abuser. Apart from sexual abuse, there are numerous kinds of abuse at different levels. There are also some self-inflicted wounds that ensnare us.

If you are the victim, you did nothing wrong, you are not at fault, you need help and protection from the abuser. I must say as a victim, your lack of action or silence will hinder and, or, delay your God-ordained purpose in life. As a result, some areas of your life, including other relationships in your life are usually, and will be affected.

*Beauty for Ashes* provides thoughts straight from God's Word that will put you on the path to victorious living in Christ. Above all else God wants us to trust Him with our darkest secrets: "God is our refuge and strength, an ever-present help in trouble." He is not a careless God.

In *Beauty for Ashes*, the reader will see that when God allows difficulties to come into your life, He equips you fully to handle them. That you can relax in His Presence, trusting in His strength.

My intention is to draw the reader's attention to the Mighty God we serve, and how He chooses to use weak ones like you and I to accomplish His purposes. Your weakness is designed to open you up to His Power. Therefore, do not fear your limitations or measure the day's demands against your strength. And that what He requires of you is to stay connected to Him. When Our greatest counsellor is our helper, the Holy Spirit. It encourages whosoever believes in Jesus' Name to walk in God's will. Whether you are the victim or the abuser, God through His only Son Jesus Christ has provided us a way out and eternal life. The Bible is one long story of God meeting our sin with His salvation, our failure with His favor, our guilt with His grace and our badness with His goodness. God gives us *Beauty for Ashes*.

Only God's love can cut through the violence and anger of our lives. When we believe that we're fine just the way we are, sin remains. Only the knife's edge of "You're okay, but only because I love you," can perform the necessary surgery on our hearts. Christ comes for the undeserving, for the sinner, for the far from okay. In His saving work, though, He becomes God's love for us, creating us anew, and making us so much more than okay. Today "It's okay," not because you're okay, but because you are loved in Christ.

*Beauty for Ashes* encourages the reader according to Scriptures and my own real life experiences. Our first break outs must occur within our own minds; when you break through in your mind, believing you can rise higher and overcome obstacles, then God will unleash the power within that will enable you to go beyond the ordinary into the extraordinary life you were designed to live.

Every person including you has seeds of greatness planted within by the Creator. When we pray bold prayers, filled with faith and inspiration, God will empower us to break out and break free, so we can believe bigger, increase our productivity, improve our relationships, and accomplish our dreams.

For the struggle to cease and the cycle to be broken, it is vital to recall, identify, confront and conquer yesterday's pain with the power of the Word of God! (Romans 12:1-2) My aim is to inspire the reader to look forward to their time with the Lord. Experience a deeper relationship with Jesus as you savor the presence of the One who understands you perfectly and loves you forever.

Today, remember that when God looks at you - when you fear that He sees only the unlovable you that you see in the mirror - He sees only His holy and righteous Son, Christ Jesus and Him crucified. God offers a choice and direction in Scripture, (*see Deuteronomy 30:19*), the Bible is a witness to God making it down to the worst people, meeting our rebellion with His rescue; our sin with His salvation; our failure with His favor; our guilt with His grace; and our badness with His goodness. On the Cross, Christ's righteousness was given to us and our sin was laid upon Him. God's "I love you," aimed at His perfect Son, is ours forever. God gives us *Beauty for Ashes*.

# TABLE OF CONTENTS

PREFACE .................................................................................. iv
INTRODUCTION ...................................................................... 10
CHAPTER ONE ........................................................................ 13
My Story ................................................................................... 13
CHAPTER TWO ....................................................................... 18
Conquer Your Pain with the Power of the Word ....................... 18
CHAPTER THREE .................................................................... 28
No Curse without cause ............................................................ 28
CHAPTER FOUR ...................................................................... 32
Defining Moments: From The Beginning To The End .............. 32
CHAPTER FIVE ........................................................................ 45
His Everlasting Love ................................................................ 45
CHAPTER SIX .......................................................................... 47
In Prison .................................................................................... 47
CHAPTER SEVEN .................................................................... 58
God Is Your Answer ................................................................. 58
CHAPTER EIGHT ..................................................................... 76
Pray Without Ceasing ............................................................... 76
CHAPTER NINE ....................................................................... 80
Knowing the Lord ..................................................................... 80
CHAPTER TEN ......................................................................... 83
The Battle of Your Mind .......................................................... 83
CHAPTER ELEVEN .................................................................. 86

Awaiting Rescue ............................................................................ 86
CHAPTER TWELVE ................................................................... 89
Just Come ...................................................................................... 89
CHAPTER THIRTEEN ............................................................... 113
God Is A Restorer ....................................................................... 113
Our Worship, Praise and Thanksgiving ..................................... 119
CHAPTER FOURTEEN .............................................................. 127
The Gospel .................................................................................. 127
CHAPTER FIFTEEN ................................................................... 134
A New Way of Life .................................................................... 134
CHAPTER SIXTEEN ................................................................... 143
Christ's Hands And Feet ............................................................. 143
CHAPTER SEVENTEEN ............................................................ 148
Molds, Our False Ideas & Mirrors .............................................. 148
CHAPTER EIGHTEEN ................................................................ 153
Empowered To Succeed ............................................................. 153
CHAPTER NINETEEN ................................................................ 173
Loved By Him In Christ ............................................................. 173

# INTRODUCTION

Sexual abuse is a topic that is not talked about enough. In fact, most people feel uncomfortable with the idea of discussing sexual abuse, whether or not they have been directly affected. However, I believe that this type of abuse, like any other type, should be spoken about so that victims of sexual abuse can begin the healing process. As the general public becomes more informed, not only on this subject, the purpose of this books is to reveal the inner healing provided through Salvation in Christ, and the transforming power of the Word of God that works mightily through His Spirit to those who believe.

*"In the beginning was the Word, and the Word was with God, and the Word was God. He was with God in the beginning. Through him all things were made; without him nothing was made that has been made. In him was life, and that life was the light of all mankind. The light shines in the darkness, and the darkness has not overcome it." (John 1:1-5 & V.12)*

*Beauty for Ashes* also acknowledges and gives thanksgiving to God for the many ways He uses other people to counsel His children, and to help us grow...and yet that Christ Himself is the Answer to our hang-ups, the one Source who can meet our deepest needs. He is wonderful in counsel and mighty in power. It is He that heals from the inside out.

Recall a time when you did something and only later became aware that it was wrong. Take a moment now to confess it to God.

"Father God, I know Your law is what is best for me. Help me to see the right path before I take the wrong one; tune my inner ear so I can more clearly hear Your guiding voice. Please forgive me for those times when I have blindly charged down the wrong paths. Amen."

God loves you in spite of your flaws and has plans to bless you. Understand this: you can read the Bible, go to church, keep all the rules-and not really know God's faithfulness, His love, and His plan for you. Until you really know God, you'll have no anchor in life; you'll be tossed to and fro by every circumstance, emotion and temptation. But when you know *Whose* you are, you'll begin to understand *who* you are, *what* you are supposed to do, and *where* you're supposed to be.

Satan has a set date to destroy you, he only comes to kill to steal and to destroy God's children; **"The thief comes only to steal and kill and destroy; I have come that they may have life, and have it to the full,"(John 10:10)**. God has a plan and a purpose for our lives to conform us to the image of His Son Jesus Christ. Prayers move God! And when God moves, people and situations change! (Luke 31:32 NKJV)PG5 **Jesus told Peter, "Satan has asked for you, that he may sift you as wheat. But I have prayed for you, that your faith should not fail*; and when you have returned to Me, strengthen your brethren,"* (Luke31:32 NKJV)** *Emphasis mine*.

Ruth and Warren Myers write: "Thank God, for the Holy Spirit---the Spirit of wisdom and understanding, the Spirit of counsel and strength. He is in you to enlighten you through His Word, to flush away your anxieties and fears, your resentments and hostilities, your guilt and regrets, as water flushes away dirt and trash… to keep you filled with Himself and to flood your heart with His love… to produce through you the fruit of love, joy, peace, patience, kindness, goodness, faithfulness, gentleness and self-control…and to enable you to give thanks for all things as hours and days and weeks pass. Rejoice that God is able to do far more than all you ask or think, according to His power that is at work within you---the same power that raised Jesus from the dead!"

**"Do you not know? Have you not heard? The LORD is the everlasting God, the Creator of the ends of the earth. He**

will not grow tired or weary, and his understanding no one can fathom. He gives strength to the weary and increases the power of the weak. Even youths grow tired and weary, and young men stumble and fall; but those who hope in the LORD will renew their strength. They will soar on wings like eagles; they will run and not grow weary; they will walk and not be faint." (Isaiah 40:28-31)

# CHAPTER ONE

# My Story

At thirteen years of age, I was raped by two men. When they released me, I was so scared and helpless. I also felt sick to my stomach…upset and confused. I painfully got up on my feet after the trauma. I was blinded by tears and could barely see where I was going. I felt dirty and violated. I was no longer a virgin I remember thinking, as tears rolled down my face. Those two men were old enough to be my father.

There are many victims of sexual abuse who suffer silently. Young girls and boys, teenage boys and teenage girls suffer as victims. There are also many adults who endure sexual abuse, and likewise suffer silently at the hands of their abuser. Apart from sexual abuse, there are numerous kinds of abuse at different levels. There are also some self-inflicted wounds that ensnare us that we need to be rescued from, as well as deliverance from generational curses – substance abuse and emotional distress.

Nonetheless, any kind of abuse is wrong and needs to be eradicated. Only the blood of Jesus Christ will bring healing from the inside out. There are ways people can get protection from abuse and we also have Professional Christian Counsellors. You have to first of all admit you are ***abusive***, or that ***you are being abused*** because that is simply unacceptable, and that is ***never*** okay. If you are the victim, you did nothing wrong, you are not at fault, you need help and protection from the abuser. I must say as a victim, your lack of action or silence will hinder and, or, delay your God-ordained purpose in life. As a result, some areas of your life, including other relationships in your life are usually, and will be, affected. **"When my heart was grieved and my spirit embittered, I was senseless and ignorant; I was a brute beast before you. Yet I am always with you; you hold me by my**

**right hand. You guide me with your counsel, and afterward you will take me into glory. Whom have I in heaven but you? And earth has nothing I desire besides you. My flesh and my heart may fail, but God is the strength of my heart and my portion forever. (Psalm 73:21-26)**

Not only did Jesus bear our sins on Calvary, but He also bore our transgressions and iniquities. This is what is passed down through the bloodline. Sin goes from being a sin to an iniquity – something that is practiced over and over again until it becomes spontaneous. Given certain circumstances or the "right" environment, you will "bend" in that direction. If the family tree is not cleansed of this iniquity, then each generation becomes worse and will do what their parents, grand-parents and great-grandparents did. The next generation will bend in the same way of the past generations and it becomes a bond of iniquity or "a generational curse".

**"Yet it pleased the Lord to bruise him; he hath put him to grief: when thou shalt make his soul an offering for sin, he shall see his seed, he shall prolong his days, and the pleasure of the Lord shall prosper in his hands. He shall see of the travail of his soul, and shall be satisfied: by his knowledge shall my righteous servant justify many; for he shall bear their iniquities.**

**Therefore will I divide him a portion with the great, and he shall divide the spoil with the strong; because he hath poured out his soul unto death: and he was numbered with the transgressors; and he bare the sin of many, and made intercession for the transgressors." (Isaiah 53:10-12).**

You may lose life and limb, sacrifice reputation and relevance, but the Gospel remains God's power to set captives free! Today, remember that when God looks at you - when you fear that He sees only the unlovable you that you see in the mirror - He sees only His holy and righteous Son, Christ Jesus and Him crucified.

## God is Our Refuge

The abuser always threatens to kill you and your family if you tell. But that is not true. This threat is so you can cooperate with them; it is just to scare you. Please tell someone, a parent, a teacher, a trusted relative. Above all else God wants us to trust Him with our darkest secrets: **"God is our refuge and strength, an ever-present help in trouble. Therefore we will not fear, though the earth give way and the mountains fall into the heart of the sea, though its waters roar and foam and the mountain quake with their surging. There is a river whose streams make glad the city of God, the holy place where the Most High dwells. God is within her she will not fall; God will help her at break of day. Nations are in uproar, kingdoms fall; he lifts his voice, the earth melts. V.10 He says; "Be still and know that I am God; I will be exalted among the nations, I will be exalted among the earth." (Psalm 46:1-6 & v.10)**

Our greatest counsellor is our helper, the Holy Spirit. There are also Christian Counsellors who are quite effective in this area because they stand on God's truth and implement His Word to bring inner healing and deliverance by using Godly principles. Whether you are the victim or the abuser, God through His only Son Jesus Christ has provided us a way out and eternal life. **"For God so loved the world, that he gave his only begotten Son, that whosoever believeth in him should not perish, but have everlasting life." (John 3:16)**

If you are the abuser remember that the more you focus on your need to get better, the worse you actually get - you become neurotic and self-absorbed. Preoccupation with our performance over Christ's performance for us actually hinders spiritual growth because it makes us increasingly self-centered and morbidly introspective-the exact opposite of how the Bible describes what it means to be sanctified. Sanctification is forgetting about yourself. **As J.C. Kromsigt said, "The good seed cannot flourish when it is repeatedly dug up for the purpose of examining its growth."**

The Bible is not a witness to the best people making it up to God; it's a witness to God making it down to the worst people. The Bible is one long story of God meeting our sin with His salvation; our failure with His favor; our guilt with His grace and our badness with His goodness. ***God gives us Beauty for Ashes.***

As mentioned above, at the tender age of thirteen, I was raped by two older men. When they released me, I felt scared and helpless. I didn't know where I was and didn't have courage to ask anyone for directions. I grew up in a Christian home, where prayer was a daily routine. Although, I felt broken, in my heart I prayed. "Father, please lead me home; I don't know where I am. AND HE DID!"

***"Your righteousness is like the highest mountains, your justice like the great deep. You, LORD, preserve both people and animals. How priceless is your unfailing love, O God! People take refuge in the shadow of your wings. For with you is the fountain of life; in your light we see light." (Psalm 36:5-6 & V. 9).***

Only God's love can cut through the violence and anger of our lives. When we believe that we're fine just the way we are, sin remains. Only the knife's edge of *"you're okay, but only because I love you"* can perform the necessary surgery on our hearts. Christ comes for the undeserving, for the sinner, for the far from okay. In His saving work, though, He becomes God's love for us, creating us anew, and making us so much more than okay. Today "it's okay," not because you're okay, but because you are loved in Christ. The Scriptures are filled with promises for help in adversity:

***"And He said to me, 'My grace is sufficient for you, for My strength is made perfect in weakness" (2 Corinthians 12:9).***

I got through the pain, the nightmares, and the helplessness by mentally separating from the body, as if the rape had happened to someone else. Over the years, I've read, watched crimes of these very tragic victims of abuse and rape reported on television, and even read in newspapers without acknowledging the reality of my experience to myself and before God for healing. Every story is different. Last year however, for the very first time I opened up to my daughter…it kind of all just came out. What the devil meant for evil, God is using it for my good and for yours as well, to His glory.

Our first break outs must occur within our own minds: when you break through in your mind, believing you can rise higher and overcome obstacles, then God will unleash the power within that will enable you to go beyond the ordinary into the extraordinary life you were designed to live. That same week I started to write my second book: *Beauty for Ashes*. Glory to God!

**"But God, who is rich in mercy, for his great love wherewith he loved us, even when we were dead in sins, hath quickened us together with Christ, (by grace ye are saved ;) And hath raised us up together, and made us sit together in heavenly places in Christ Jesus: That in the ages to come he might show the exceeding riches of his grace in his kindness toward us through Christ Jesus. For by grace are ye saved through faith: and that not of yourselves: it is the gift of God: Not of works, lest any man should boast. For we are his workmanship, created in Christ Jesus unto good works, which God hath before ordained that we should walk in them." (Ephesians 2:4-9)**

God already knows every need and every concern you have. He knows the number of hairs on your head. Be open and honest and tell God how you feel, but don't turn that into self-pity session, that will only make you more discouraged. Every person including you has seeds of greatness planted within by the Creator. When we pray bold prayers, filled with faith and inspiration, God will empower us to break out and break free, so we can believe bigger, increase our productivity, improve our relationships, and accomplish our dreams.

# CHAPTER TWO

## Conquer Your Pain with the Power of the Word

For the struggle to cease and the cycle to be broken, *it is vital to recall, identify, confront and conquer yesterday's pain with the power of the Word of God!* **(Romans 12:1-2)** Sadly, this rape ended in pregnancy and thereafter, I had an abortion. Even after praying and asking for forgiveness from God, I still struggled with forgiving myself. With God's knowledge comes understanding. The Bible says that when God looks at us, He sees His Son! He's not fooled. Jesus Christ is God Himself! But we get sovereignly covered with the righteousness of the One to whom God shows partiality. Wearing our normal clothes, we're in trouble. Clothed with Christ, though, we partake in all the glory that comes with being the favorite. Not because of who you are, but because of who ransomed us and who paid for our freedom from the tyranny of trying so hard to be accepted, and always worried that we haven't done enough. *"Not the smallest letter, not the least stroke of a pen" (Matt. 5:18)* will be changed. When our sin causes us to become less and less of what God created us to be, because we were fearfully and wonderfully made to live for so much more, God is grievingly angry. *(Mark 3:1-5)*

So often we are merely angry at the sins we see in others and at the state of the world, sure things are not the way they are supposed to be, but Jesus in John 16:33 said; "I have told you these things, so that you may have peace. In this world you will have trouble. But take heart! I have overcome the world." Your path through this world has many ups and downs. Your down times are difficult, but they serve an important purpose. Pain and struggle help you change and grow stronger when you trust Jesus in the midst of adversity. Your troubles are comparable to a woman enduring labor pains. Her suffering is very real, and she may wonder how much longer she can bear the pains. However, this arduous struggle produces a wonderful result---a newborn baby. While you labor through your earthly struggles, keep your eyes on the promised reward: boundless Joy in heaven! A grieving anger can contain compassion and hope for a world that so desperately needs a Savior. In Christ, that Savior has come. Christ came into a world that was not the way it was supposed to be—locked into self-centeredness and sin—and was angry. But His was a God-centered anger, and He took God's anger at sin onto Himself, for you and me.

    Jesus offers forgiveness full and free; this is the hardest thing for most of us believers. We hang on to our guilt and shame, forgetting that in **Micah 7:19** and **Psalm 103:12** our Lord practices a *"forgetfulness"* for the repentant person's sin. If you are a Christian, you are right now under the completely sufficient imputed righteousness of Christ. Your pardon is full and final. In Christ, you're forgiven. When you bring your sin up in conviction to Him, it's as if He says, "What sin?" Following repentance, union with Christ is set forth in the principles of the allegory of the vine and the branches in John 15. ***"I am the true vine, and the Father is the gardener. He cuts off every branch in me that bears no fruit, while every branch that does bear fruit he prunes so that it will be even more fruitful. You are already clean because of the word I have spoken to you..." (See John 15).*** This teaching by Jesus shows us how to abide in the living Son of God daily-even hourly.

    Where can you find relief? Alcohol, drugs, relationships, work, money, sex, etc.? This kind of relief won't work long-term, you probably already know that. The Bible says, *"Anxiety in a man's heart weighs it down,"* causing hopelessness and depression. Satan is sometimes the source of anxiety and depression. People can contribute to your anxiety and depression, and seemingly "good" people can be used by evil spirits. They can make you want to live—or die! (See Pr. 18:21 NIV) Our pride and disobedience also allow Satan to invade our thoughts and emotions. But by humbling ourselves and aligning our will with God's will, we invite Him to reverse Satan's assault, overcoming our anxiety and depression. ***"... God resisteth the proud, but giveth grace unto the humble. Submit yourselves therefore to God. Resist the devil, and he will flee from you." (James 4:6-8)***

Circumstances do not dictate our responses but that which lies within us. Two influences will be found in every believer's heart: God's grace *and* remaining sin. Therefore, the call for real, and radical, practical change in our lives is laid out for us in*: (2 Peter 1.)* This chapter reflects the Spirit's work that the apostle Paul taught in **Romans 8**, May you and I, by God's grace, be enabled to make the real changes of character and habit as they are mapped out in this chapter.

Trial and adversity are powerful forces in life. Satan's work surely is to lure and tempt us with the things of the world and the flesh. *(See Ephesians 4; 14-15 & 17-19, 23, 26 & 27)*) In *Ephesians 6* we read of the armor of God that equips us to stand firm, press forward, and fight the good fight of faith. Greater is He that is in you than He that is in the world. But the work of the Spirit in the lives of believers is opened up to us in Romans 7 and 8. The Spirit Himself enables us to grasp the reality of how He prevails in our lives when we abide in Christ and engage in a heartfelt trust in Him.

It is absolutely vital to read and study the Word of God. *"In the beginning was the Word, and the Word was with God, and the Word was God. He was with God in the beginning. Through him all things were made In him was life, and that life was the light of all mankind. The light shines in the darkness, and the darkness has not overcome it. The Word became flesh and made his dwelling among us. We have seen his glory, the glory of the one and only Son, who came from the Father, full of grace and truth." (John 1:1-5 & 14)*

**Jesus Is the Word!** Take hold of the hope that God has offered you be encouraged. Notice, however, that "take hold" is an active verb---requiring effort on your part. *(Hebrews 6:18)* As the apostle Paul taught, you need to press on toward the goal and live up to what you have already attained. This requires you to exert yourself—grasping onto the heavenly hope from which so many blessings flow. (Philippians 3:14-16) One of those blessings is encouragement. Be encouraged is a passive form of the verb. You receive encouragement as a free gift from God when you make the effort to hold on to your hope—focusing on the finished works of Jesus Christ on the Cross, His living presence in you and His promise to take you to heaven *Galatians 2:20*. The inward worship of the soul described in **Ephesians 3:14-21** can blossom in our lives, through which a refreshing, rejuvenating fountain flows and through which we experience an intimate fellowship with God Our Father, never losing sight of the glory and the worthiness of our God.

There are also some self-inflicted wounds that ensnare us that we need to be rescued from. These can be generational curses, substance abuse and emotional distress. Not only did Jesus bear our sins on Calvary, but He also bore our transgressions and iniquities. This is what is passed down through the blood line. Sin goes from being a sin to an iniquity – something that is practiced over and over again until it becomes spontaneous, it becomes "a generational curse". Today, remember that when God looks at you - when you fear that He sees only the unlovable you that you see in the mirror - He sees only His holy and righteous Son, Christ Jesus and Him crucified. God offers a choice and direction in Scripture, See *Deuteronomy 30:19.* The Bible is a witness to God making it down to the worst people, meeting our rebellion with His rescue; our sin with His salvation; our failure with His favor; our guilt with His grace; our badness with His goodness. ***God gives us Beauty for Ashes.***

To this day, I believe a miracle took place, I never asked anyone for any directions to get home. I just followed my God given instincts and kept walking. I have no idea to this day how I got home, but by the grace of God I did! My parents weren't home from work when I got there. I never did tell them about the rape. **"Your love, LORD, reaches to the heavens, your faithfulness to the skies. Your righteousness is like the highest mountains, your justice like the great deep. You, LORD, preserve both people and animals." (Psalm 36:5-7)**

This rape resulted in a pregnancy and thereafter an abortion. I was tormented over the abortion for a long time because I felt I was just as evil as the rapists. Many times, I cried out to the Lord for forgiveness. It's one thing to ask for forgiveness, but do you believe God has forgiven you? Better yet, have you forgiven yourself for your part in the wrong-doing? I was young and did not know any better, but that is the exact and perfect tool the devil needed to torment me. That lie kept me from believing that God's forgiveness is final, and that what Christ did on the Cross is perfectly perfect and completely complete...and that through Christ and His blood, I am "all" right as a person, now and forever: totally clean, every stain removed and totally forgiven. What amazing grace!

The Christian's self-esteem is ultimately that person's individual judgment about their worthiness in Christ. Your reputation lies in the truth that you have been saved and belong to God, that you have been equipped in Christ to face any situation of life and overcome it, and that you are lovable because Christ first loved you. You are forgiven of all past sins and you are not a product of your past. You are capable of walking in newness of life because the Holy Spirit has promised to be with you constantly as your Guide, Comforter and Teacher.

The devil was busy accusing me in my mind; BUT GOD!!!...The Judge to whom I am accountable as the final Authority, the Chief Justice of the Supreme Court of all the Earth...said, and His word cannot be broken...No condemnation now hangs over the head of those who are in Christ Jesus. **"Therefore, there is now no condemnation for those who are in Christ Jesus, because through Christ Jesus the law of the Spirit who gives life has set you free from the law of sin and death."(Romans 8:1-2)** The Judge, Himself, set me free, for those the Son sets free are free indeed! (John) Then, and then only was I able to forgive myself. All the glory goes to God! You have to have knowledge of what the Word of God says otherwise, the devil will continue to harass you and to use the past negatives as weapons against you to tear you down.

**"So justice is far from us, and righteousness does not reach us. We look for light, but all is darkness; for brightness, but we walk in deep shadows. Like the blind we grope along the wall, feeling our way like people without eyes. At midday we stumble as if it were twilight; among the strong, we are like the dead. We all growl like bears; we moan mournfully like doves. We look for justice but there is none; for deliverance, but it is far away. For our offenses are many in your sight, and**

our sins testify against us. Our offenses are ever with us, and we acknowledge our iniquities: rebellion and treachery against the LORD, turning our backs on our God, inciting revolt and oppression, uttering lies our hearts have conceived. So justice is driven back, and righteousness stands at a distance; truth has stumbled in the streets, honesty cannot enter. Truth is nowhere to be found, and whoever shuns evil becomes a prey. "The LORD looked and was displeased that there was no justice. He saw that there was no justice. He saw that there was no one, he was appalled that there was no one to intervene; so his own arm achieved salvation for him, and his own righteousness sustained him." (Psalm 59: 9-16)

My favorite illustration of our relationship to the law in Christ comes from Paul Zahl's *Who Will Deliver Us?*

"[We are] a little like the duck hunter who was hunting with his friend in a wide-open barren land in southern Georgia. Far away on the horizon he noticed a cloud of smoke. Soon, he could hear the sound of crackling. A wind came up and he realized the terrible truth: a brush fire was advancing his way. It was moving so fast that he and his friend could not outrun it. The hunter began to rifle through his pockets. Then he emptied all the contents of his knapsack. To his friend's amazement, he pulled out a match and struck it. He lit a small fire around the two of them. Soon they were standing in a circle of blackened earth, waiting for the brush fire to come. They did not have to wait long. They covered their mouths with handkerchiefs and braced themselves. The fire came near-and swept over them. But they were completely unhurt. They weren't even touched. Fire would not burn the place where fire had already burned."

The point here is that the law is like a brush fire that takes no prisoners. It cannot be escaped or extinguished or circumvented. But if we stand in the *burned-over place*, where law has already done its worst, we will not get hurt. Its power has not been nullified nor has its necessity and authority been denied. Yet because of where we are standing, not a hair on our heads will be singed. *The death of Christ is the burned –over place*. There we huddle, hardly believing, yet relieved. Christ's death has armed the law, and where there was once guilt, now all that remains is gratitude.

The Gospel declares that Jesus came, not to abolish the Law, but to fulfill it- Jesus met all of God's holy conditions so that our relationship with God could be wholly unconditional. The demand maker became a demand keeper and died for me - a law breaker. **"Do not think that I came to abolish the Law or the prophets; I have not come to abolish them but to fulfill them." (Matthew 5:17)**

Some victims of childhood or, any sexual abuse, often experience long-lasting effects of the incident. Sometimes the effects are not acknowledged for years, and suddenly surface at a later point in the individual's life. Some children have suffered sexual abuse under adult family members. Being sexually abused by an adult also violates a child's trust, making the child wary of adults in general, even though these are people that the child should trust and count on.

Today, remember that when God looks at you- when you fear that He sees only the unlovable you that you see in the mirror, He sees only His holy and righteous Son. The Gospel is that Jesus has died to save sinners like me, you, the sexual abusers, murderers, liars, thieves, fornicators, gossipers, hypocrites, and whatever your ultimate no, no is…in short, we were all shapen in iniquity, we all have sinned and gone astray. There are no exceptions. **"For all have sinned and fall short of the glory of God." (Romans 3:23)**. So, the Law serves us by showing us how to love God and others. But we fail to do this every day. And when we fail, it is the Gospel that brings comfort by reminding us that God's infinite approval of us doesn't depend on our keeping of the Law, but on Christ's keeping of the Law for us. And guess what? This makes me want to obey Him more, not less!

Jesus came to Earth to be grace in the face of the world's judgment, to be love in the face of the world's critique, to be the gospel in the face of the Law, and to be God's yes to us. Jesus came to Earth to **"bring good news to the oppressed, to bind up the broken hearted, to proclaim liberty to the captives, and to**

**release to the prisoners; to proclaim the year of the LORD's favor," (Isa.61:1-2).** Praise the LORD!

Why does the "abuser" get to walk away free? Does he? *Once we release those that have done wrong to us by forgiving them, it becomes God's business, but this is what He tells us*; **"Do not repay anyone evil for evil. Be careful to do what is right in the eyes of everyone. If it is possible, as far as it depend on you, live at peace with everyone. Do not take revenge, my dear friends, but leave room for God's wrath, for it is written: 'It is mine to avenge; I will repay,' says the Lord. On the contrary: 'If your enemy is hungry, feed him; if he is thirsty, give him something to drink. In doing this, you will hip burning coals on his head.' Do not be overcome by evil, but overcome evil with good. (Romans 12:17-21)** Our only part as believers is to forgive, remember; **"Very rarely will anyone die for a righteous person, though for a good person someone might possibly dare to die, But God demonstrates his own love for us like this: While we were yet still sinners, Christ died for us,"(Romans 5:7-8)**. God requires that we forgive others, for our own good. **"Bear with each other and forgive one another if any of you has a grievance against someone. Forgive as the Lord forgave you," (Col.3:13).** It takes the grace of God to be able to apply the process of forgiveness in most circumstances. **"So watch yourselves. If your brother or your sister sins against you, rebuke them; and if they repent, forgive them. Even if they sin against you seven times in a day and seven times come back to you saying, 'I repent,' you must forgive them," (Luke 17:3-4).** There's just no way around this one. God demands it!

Victims of rape frequently blame themselves; most often they feel guilty, ashamed and angry. Like I expressed in earlier chapters, these feelings are frequently turned inward, their memories of abuse are often repressed through the very same mechanism, which enables the child, teenager or whatever age you were when it happened...to survive the horror: dissociation. He or she gets through the betrayal, the physical assault, the pain and the helplessness by mentally separating from the body. It seems as though the abuse is happening to someone else. **"Your**

**righteousness, God, reaches to the heavens, you who have done great things. Who is like you God? Though you have made me see troubles, many and bitter, you will restore my life again; from the depth of the earth you will again bring me up. You will increase my honor and comfort me once again."(Psalm 71:19-21**).

Your need moves God's heart, but your faith moves Him to action. When your life is turned over to God, when you do what God tells you to do and when you go where He sends you, you move from the natural realm to the supernatural one. **"But the advocate, the Holy Spirit, whom the Father will send in my name, will teach you all things and will remind you of everything I have said to you. Peace I leave with you, my peace I give you. I do not give to you as the world gives. Do not let your hearts be troubled and do not be afraid," (John 14:26-27).** Though the battle is fierce, and you are weak, your resources in God are unlimited. His Spirit is ever ready to help you; you have only to ask. Remember that this Holy Helper is infinitely powerful and infinitely loving. And He's eager to help you. Call upon Him with confident trust, for His unfailing love surrounds you. **"Many are the woes of the wicked, but the LORD's unfailing love surrounds the man who trusts in him," (Psalm 32:10).** God not only has a *plan* for your life He has a *place* for it. Yes, you must have the right *strategy*, but you must also be in the right *spot*. **"I am the Lord your God, who teaches you what is best for you, (Isaiah 48:17NIV).** If your heart's desire is to honor God in all things, He will show you the best location to succeed in. Indeed, He will go ahead of you and rearrange circumstances to your advantage. He did for Abraham. **"By faith Abraham when called to go to a place he would later receive as his inheritance, obeyed and went, even though he did not know where he was going," (Heb.11:8 NIV).**

Ask God for direction in your life, every step of the way, He will show you where to go, this is not always easy. There were times I did want to go, or even wondered if it indeed was the Lord instructing me. "I felt like, why can't He bless me right here, right now!" Remember, it's not by your might nor by your power, but by the Spirit of God. He will lead you in all truth. *God is the potter and you are the clay, so trust and obey Him.* Thy word have I hid in my heart that I may not sin against thee...hearing and hearing therefore becomes a vital practice if we are to fight these fleshly tendencies in our daily battle in our mind. **"I will instruct you and teach you in the way you should go; I will counsel you with my loving eye on you. Do not be like the horse or the mule, which have no understanding but must be controlled by bit and bridle or they will not come to you. Many are the woes of the wicked, but the LORD's unfailing love surrounds the one who trusts in him." (Psalm 32:8-10)**.

If we are honest with ourselves, we are frequently aware that our spiritual understanding is dim and hazy. This darkness, which is the natural realm of our mind and senses, is the element of spiritual blindness. But God says; **"Thou wilt keep in perfect peace, whose mind is stayed on thee: because he trusteth in thee. Trust ye in the LORD forever: for in the LORD JEHOVAH is everlasting strength," (Isaiah 26:3)**. It is a state that may make us feel that we are alone and destitute. It is the embodiment of all our negative feelings and desires. And, though we may have glimpses of vision of His peace and perfection, we are prone to again and again sink in the depth of doubt, even while the splendor of God's reality is all around us. This is part of our journey, our existence, our meaning, as human beings on God's Earth.

# CHAPTER THREE

## No Curse without cause

Author Paula White in her Book, *How to Reap Blessings and Break Curses,* has written: "Some abusers learned to abuse from their parents. Their early history consisted of receiving abuse themselves and or seeing others abused (one abusing the other or their sibling, etc.). As a consequence, abuse is the normal condition of life for these people. Such people internalized a particular relationship dynamic, namely the complementary roles of "abuser" and "victim". They are familiar with and fully understand the terror of being the helpless victim from their own childhood experience. As they become adults, they simply turn this relationship dynamic around and start acting out their "abuser" side of the relationship dynamic they have learned. By choosing to be the aggressor and abuser, they may get their first sense of taking control over their own destiny and not being at the mercy of others. That they hurt others in the process may go unregistered or only occur as a dim part of their awareness." **"Thou shalt not bow down thyself to them, nor serve them: for I the Lord thy God am a jealous God, visiting the iniquity of the fathers upon the children unto the third and fourth generation of them that hate me; and shewing mercy unto thousands of them that love me, and keep my commandments." (Exodus 20:5-6)** If this behavior is passed down, whether sexual abuse, incest, physical abuse, verbal abuse…or a certain illness has persisted in your family tree from generation to generation whether you acknowledge this trend or not, you are living under a generational curse.

Sin means to miss the mark. We have all not committed adultery, nor gotten drunk, nor stolen, but we all have done one thing since Adam. I mentioned this earlier…We have turned to our own way, which is not God's way. God describes this as iniquity. The root problem of humanity is rebellion against God.

The Good News of the Gospel of Jesus Christ is, God has laid on Jesus the iniquity, the rebellion, of us all.

Iniquity can be thought of as the practice of sin to the point it becomes pleasurable; or a predisposition to sin. Iniquity is a weakness to yield to that particular sin that has been passed from generation-to-generation through your family bloodline. As a result, we deal with recurrent situations, or patterns of behavior in our lives, that cannot be explained solely in terms of what happened in your lifetime or personal experiences.

Sometimes, the things you fall down to really have nothing to do with you but are a predisposition you inherited from your ancestors who fell down easily to the same things! Proverbs 26:2 tells us, **"Like a flitting sparrow, like a flying swallow, so a curse without cause shall not alight," (Proverbs 26:2).** Wherever there is a curse at work, there is a cause for it. In the name of Jesus, you must identify, confront and bring the defeating patterns that have continued to derail your family for generations under the Power of the Precious Name of Jesus Christ! The blood of Jesus defeats everything. Curses result from hearing God's voice and not doing what He says. The refusal to hear and obey God's voice can be summed up in one word: REBELLION. Jesus endured in our place all the evil consequences that were due by divine justice to our iniquity. In exchange, God offers us all the good that was due to the sinless obedience of Jesus. So, why do some people who love God – never get ahead in life? You must confront and conquer the cause of the curse!"

## Identifying and Removing Generational Curses

Jacqueline: What is a generational curse? A generational curse is an uncleansed iniquity that increases in strength from one generation to next, affecting the members of that family and all who come into relationship with that family. They are cycles.

"But it shall come to pass, if thou wilt not hearken unto the voice of the Lord thy God, to observe to do all his commandments and his statutes which I command thee this day; that all these curses shall come upon thee, and overtake thee." (Deuteronomy 28:15)

The Bible makes a distinction between the term sin, transgression and iniquity. Not only did Jesus bear our sins on Calvary, but He also bore our transgressions and iniquities. This is what is passed down through the bloodline. As illustrated in the creation of the Earth in Genesis 1, everything reproduces after its own kind. We acknowledge this principle in buying a pedigreed animal, but we completely ignore this principle when we deal with people.

**<u>Are you and your family affected by a generational curse?</u>**

1) Have a pattern of constant failure?
2) Have a history of untimely deaths, suicides or a large number of people who have died prematurely?
3) Exhibit a high level of anger or wrath?
4) Have a high record of accidents or accidents that are unusual in nature?
5) Have a history of abuse such as physical, emotional, or sexual?
6) Have a history of chronic illness or disease?
7) Have a history of mental illness that may have progressed through generations?
8) Exhibit any of these personality behaviors: high-control; manipulation, addiction, co-dependency, depression, unforgiveness, addictions, or social isolation?

Since the transgression of Adam, all families came under a curse. However, God made provision. (See Isaiah 53:10-12)

For the struggle to cease and the cycle of generational curses to be broken, first allow the Holy Spirit to bring to your remembrance the sins and iniquities of your forefathers and your parents. And then begin with acknowledgement, then repentance of the iniquities of your forefathers, then appropriation and application of the blood of Jesus! The blood of Jesus Christ defeats everything. One of the main vehicles of both generational blessings and curses is words! (See Jas. 3:5, 8) You hide yourself from the enemies in your life by speaking God's Word. When you speak the Word of God over yourself, you are establishing yourself. His Word causes you to be stable and not waver. Speak His Word…it breaks the curse!

# CHAPTER FOUR

## Defining Moments: From The Beginning To The End

There are defining moments that made you the person you are. Regardless of whether we are female or male, I am sure that we all know that deep desire that just can't seem to be filled that extends from rejection or an injury to our soul that we barely understand. This is the place of vulnerability, that's why we must cast our burdens unto the Lord, for He cares for us.

The Scripture also tells us not to be conformed to this world **"I beseech you brethren, by the mercies of God, that ye present your bodies a living sacrifice, holy, acceptable unto God, which is your reasonable service. And be not conformed to this world: but be ye transformed by the renewing of your mind, that ye may prove what is that good and acceptable and perfect will of God. (Romans 12:1-2)** I thank my gracious and sovereign God that He has been with me and carried me from the day of my birth until today. God has known my whole life and yours, from beginning to end, since before we were born. God wrote in His book all the days that He ordained for me before one of them came to be. God knows each one of us in our brokenness, but He has promised never to leave us nor to forsake us.

In all our distresses, the Lord Jesus was distressed as well. **"You have searched me, LORD, and you know me. You know when I sit and when I rise; you perceive my thoughts from afar. You discern my going out and my lying down; you are familiar with all my ways. Before a word is on my tongue you, LORD, know it completely. You hem me in behind and before, and you lay your hand upon me. Such knowledge is too wonderful for me, too lofty for me to attain. Where can I go from your Spirit? Where can I flee from your presence? If I go up to the heaven, you are there. If I rise on the wings of the dawn, if I settle on the far side of the sea, even there your hand**

**will guide me, your right hand will hold me fast. If I say, "Surely the darkness will hide me," even the darkness will not be dark to you; the night will shine like the day, for darkness is as light to you. For you created my inmost being; you knit me together in my mother's womb. I praise you because I am fearfully and wonderfully made; your works are wonderful, I know that full well. My frame was not hidden from you when I was made in the secret place, when I was woven in the depth of the earth.** *Your eyes saw my unformed body; all the days ordained for me were written in your book before one of them came to be.* **How precious to me are your thoughts God! How vast is the sum of them!" (Psalm 139:1-17)** *(Emphasis mine)*

The hurt that you have gone through, over and over in your life can become a destruction and a hindrance, delaying the work God wants to do in your life. God wants to bring healing in the places in your life you try to run away from, or were hurt by others, thereby possibly hurting others as a result of being hurt yourself. These behaviors manifest by either being self-destructive, cold, bitter or over indulging in "things" that can never fully bring the healing that needs to take place from the core root of the real problem. It's the shed blood of Jesus Christ that will eradicate these struggles and your faith in the Word of God will empower you to break out and reject any labels that might limit you. Only in Christ are we indeed able to experience true healing from the inside out in these places of pain from childhood to now and or in other unforeseen challenges occurring in our lives.

The scales of our belief are formed over a period of time through our lifetime; they are continuously being formed looking in the wrong mirror. They give us a false perspective of who we are, and therefore they hold us back and limit us. These images form wrong beliefs of our identity, the truth is only found in the mirror of Gods' Word, for the Word of God is truth; **"For the word of the LORD is right and true; he is faithful in all does." (Psalm 33:4)**

For the cycle of generational curses to be broken, it is vital to recall the inconsistent messages of your childhood, betrayal, hurt by friends or loved ones, sickness, loss and take them to the

Lord in prayer; **"Come to me, all you who are weary and burdened, and I will give you rest. Take my yoke upon you and learn from me, for I am gentle and humble in heart, and you will find rest for your souls. For my yoke is easy and my burden is light," (Matthew 11:28-30).** Like it or not, those messages may still be influencing your behavior today on an unconscious level in every area of your life. God intended the spirit-man to have dominion and to rule over the natural or carnal man, but the dysfunctional soul is carnal. That's why you must identify the inconsistent messages of your childhood and confront and crush their defeating messages with the power of the Word of God. To lay hold upon your blessing, you have to exercise your God given authority. **"Christ redeemed us from the curse of the law, having become a curse for us (for it is written, cursed is everyone who hangs on a tree), that the blessing of Abraham might come upon the Gentiles in Christ Jesus, that we might receive the promise of the Spirit through faith." (Galatians 3:13-14)**

The Word refers to carnality as everything in man that is NOT under the control or dominion of the Holy Spirit, via your own yielded spirit. The knowledge of how your current patterns were formed will help give you the tools to release you from self-critical indictments that create sick cycles and soul-ties that are ungodly.

## When You Know Better, You Live Better

Why are God's people living with lack - that is, tolerating fear anxiety, sicknesses and disease, living with stress and torment, addictive behaviors and habits- instead of experiencing what God has declared and desired for them that is a life of "wholeness?" We clearly cannot blame God. He is a God of the impossible! Obviously, the problem is not on His end. So, what is it that we might be missing? His best plan for our life. What is holding us back from living and coming in alignment with the abundant life Jesus talked about? Why can't we move into the realm that God has already established over our lives? I believe it is not that we are doing everything "wrong"…sometimes we are just not doing enough of what is "right." When you "know better, you live better."

One of the most powerful principles of God's Word is that of ***first fruits.*** It is found in Mathew 6:33, "But seek first the kingdom of God and His righteousness, and all these things shall be added to you." (NKJV)

In Paula White's Book, *First Things First*, she writes how to effectively rearrange your life through the principle of First Fruits. Here is a quote from her book; "God says first things first! You will not experience the fullness of "abundant life" and promises of God without the foundation of first fruits. It is prioritizing His presence in your life. It's the order and accurate arrangement of things. The principle of first fruits provides the foundation and structure for God's blessings in your life.

There is a pattern laid out for your success, for your well-being and abundant life. There is a pattern laid out for your peace and protection. There is a pattern laid out for your family and future. There is a pattern laid out for your career and calling. It's already been fashioned and formed by the master architect. You just have to serve in obedience to God and follow His pattern."

In the Scriptures in the book of Hosea we read: **"…my people are destroyed from lack of knowledge,"** (Hosea 4:6). Paul writing to Timothy said: **"Do your best to present yourself to God as one approved, a worker who does not need to be ashamed and who correctly handles the word of truth," (2 Timothy 3:15).** In the book of Proverbs, we are reminded that "Wisdom" is the principal thing; *therefore,* get wisdom, and with all thy getting get understanding.

God's people are not prospering in their spirit, soul and body! They are not living the fullness of what God sent His Son as a sacrifice to give us – abundant life. We see lack either in love, or joy, or finances, or health, or peace of mind, or household and family. I talk to people all the time who love the Lord and serve God faithfully, but they struggle day-to-day, week-to-week, month-to-month - just to survive. I know what that is like. I know many folks who live "paycheck-to-paycheck" fearing that at any moment something could happen that would completely wipe out their finances. These people who love God, but are often emotionally depleted and dysfunctional, stressed out, sick, fearful and all too often defeated. Many of us believers still experience these struggles, but God intends His children to live a wholesome fulfilled life to His glory.

### Choose Life That Both You and Your Seed May Live

**"I call heaven and earth to record this day against you that I have set before you life and death, blessing and cursing; and, therefore choose life that both thou and thy seed may live."(Deuteronomy 30:19)**

Although life and blessing have been provided, the choice is yours for what you will live in. In this verse, God reminded His people, *"This choice not only affects your life, but also the descendants that follow you."* The alternatives therefore are very clear, life and blessing on one hand, death and curses on the other. Your choice of life and blessings or death and curses continue from generation to generation, which is why God exhorts us to *"choose life that you and your seed may live."*

To vilify someone or something means, "to lower in estimation or importance; to utter slanderous and abusive statements against; defame." The main vehicle of both blessings and curses is WORDS. It's not what others say to you or about you, but what you say to yourself about yourself! Your future lives in your mouth, whether you choose life or death; it's a choice you make for yourself and those in your family.

**"And it shall come to pass, if thou shalt harken diligently unto the voice of the Lord thy God, to observe and to do all his commandments which I command thee this day, that the Lord thy God will set thee on high above all nations of the earth: And all these blessings shall come on thee, and overtake thee, if thou shalt hearken unto the voice of the Lord thy God," (Deuteronomy 28:1-2)**. Blessings are promised to those who hear and obey His voice! Although we are given a higher covenant, this principle is still in operation. The fact that we are in the New Testament does not mean the principle of generational blessing and cursing is done away with – Jesus came to fulfill the Law – not to do away with it. **"Think not that I am come to destroy the law, or the prophets: I am not come to destroy, but to fulfill,"(Matt.5:17)**. You can bless your family with gifts that will last for eternity when you walk in generational blessing. As you yield to the Holy Spirit's cleansing work, you overcome the weaknesses passed onto you from generations long ago. Your victory is not lost with you – but passes on through your natural and spiritual DNA. God not only blesses you for your obedience to Him...He blesses those who come after you.

### The Helper

In the book of; John 20:19-22 when Jesus, after His resurrection, breathes the Holy Spirit on the disciples; **"On the evening of that day, the first day of the week, the doors being locked where the disciples were for fear of the Jews, Jesus came and stood among them and said to them, 'Peace be with you.' When he had said this, he showed them his hands and his side. Then the disciples were glad when they saw the Lord. Jesus said to them again, 'Peace be with you. As the Father has sent me, even so I am sending you.' And when he had said this, he breathed on them and said to them, 'Receive the Holy Spirit.' "** Jesus' breathing of the Holy Spirit on His disciples recalls the Genesis account when the LORD God formed the man of the dust from the ground and breathed into his nostrils the breath of life **(Gen. 2:7)**. And also, in **Ezekiel 37:1-14** passage when the Lord drives Ezekiel to a valley full of dry bones. In that valley God causes breath to enter the bones and right before Ezekiel's eyes the lifeless bones are assembled into a huge living army. Here God does something even more climactic than before, since, "the breath is not animating a body that had yet to live. It animates bodies that were dead." Behold the beauty of the gospel of Jesus - it is the power of God: **(Ephesians 2:1-7)**

And that's why I praise God that the things that happened in my past, both enjoyable and painful, the specific family into which I was born and the opportunities God provided or did not provide, and for the things in my past that appear to be limitations, hindrances and even the wounds of old hurts, the unmet emotional needs, the mistakes or neglect of other people—even their cruelty to me, their abuse…it is good to know that, through it all, in all my distresses He was distressed. But most importantly, I thank the Lord Jesus, that on the Cross He bore my griefs and yours and carried our sorrows, as well as our sins…and therefore, I can kneel at the Cross and worship Christ Jesus, as the One who took on Himself all my pain and experienced it to the full.

I thank Him that the things that happened in my past, both enjoyable and painful, are raw materials for blessings, both in my life and in the lives of others, that I can write this book not from a place of shame but a place of victory in Christ Jesus my Lord and Savior. *God has given us Beauty for Ashes!* And so, I thank God that I can rest on His presence working in me through my Helper, the Holy Spirit, knowing that am not alone and that the battle is the Lord's. **"In everything give thanks; for this is God's will for you in Christ Jesus."(1 Thessalonians 5:18)**.

Only the truth will set us free. The Word of God is truth, the truth breaks generational curses. **"Jesus saith unto him, I am the way, the truth, and the life: no man cometh unto the Father, but by me," (John 14:6).** *When* Jesus spoke of Himself as "the truth", this Greek word literally means "reality". He was saying, "I am the reality." This Word (which He is) is the reality. Your first objective in overcoming any false message creating patterns of curses in your life is to take a good hard look at these myths and then get *reality*. Compare the myths with what the Word of God says you are and stand on it!

God is calling you to confront your Jacob. He is calling you to refocus your attention on the giver of life and healer of hearts. You cannot praise or honor God for what He has given you until you have been *weaned from the idols of your past*! Focus on tearing down your idols and worshipping the One True God who has broken the curse to redeem you.

God in His Word says; **"No weapon forged against you will prevail, and you will refute every tongue that curses you.**

**This is the heritage of the servants of the LORD, and this is their vindication from me," declares the LORD,"(Isaiah 54:17).** I thank God, that my failures and mistakes and even the hurt, struggles and challenges caused over the years are part of the "all things" that He works together for good...as well as the tensions and stresses, my hostile and anxious feelings, my regrets, my trips into shame and self-blame...and the specific things that trigger them. I praise Him that "all things," including these, can contribute to my spiritual growth and my experience of God...When my heart is overwhelmed, I'm more aware of my need to cry to Him...to take refuge in Him...to rely on Him. These things keep reminding me to depend on the Lord with all my heart...they prompt me to trust in His Love, His forgiveness, His power, His sufficiency, His ability to overrule, and His transforming presence within me.

I thank God that my shortcomings and failures bring pressure on me to open myself to God more fully, and they let Him show me deep and hidden needs: griefs and hurts that I've never exposed to His healing touch and in that same simple way, I let go of the whole burden of my life and service and rest on His presence working in me through the Holy Spirit to transform me. God wants to do the same for you. If you have never given your life to Jesus as LORD and Savior of your life, please reconsider. Please don't let this golden opportunity escape you. You can pray the prayer of Salvation right now. At the very end of this book, please read and believe every word you pray. If you prayed that prayer you are now born-again! Look for a church that's Christ-centered. Read your Bible and pray every day, if you want to grow. God will do the rest.

Make the Holy Spirit your best friend, pour out your heart to Him, learn to speak to Him and let Him lead you, you will truly be amazed! Through the transforming power of the Holy Spirit I am grateful that am I able to face and acknowledge His constant cleansing of each sin He makes me aware of. Making me able to forgive myself for things that I had been unable to forgive myself before, and then turn back to Him as my Lord, who comforts me and tells me that I am free from condemnation simply because

Christ died for me and rose again...that it doesn't depend on how well I live.

God uses our sins and failures to humble us, and this opens us to the inflow of His grace-amazing grace that enables us to hold our head high, not in pride but in humble gratitude for His underserved, unchanging love and total cleansing! **"Trust in the LORD with all your heart, and do not lean on your own understanding," (Proverbs 3:5)**

If anyone has the capacity to make it and thrive in this world—this world plagued by so much darkness, disease, and disillusionment—it is you and me. It's those of us who have received the Holy Spirit, those of us who are energized by rivers of living water. We are drawing from and being sustained by an infinite source.

As ones who are filled with God's Spirit, we must join God in speaking life and hope over this decaying and despondent world. And we must accept and invite words of hope that are spoken over us by others based on the Word of God, and we have to speak life and hope over ourselves. The Spirit within us we received because God raised Jesus from the dead. The Spirit within us teems with life and energy.

**"Son of man, can these Bones live?"**

**"Then he said to me, 'Son of man these bones are the whole house of Israel. Behold, they say, 'Our bones are dried up, and our hope is lost; we are indeed cut off. Therefore prophesy, and say to them, 'Thus says the Lord GOD: Behold, I will open your graves and raise you from your graves, O my people. And I will bring you to the land of Israel. And you shall know that I am the LORD, when l open your graves, and raise you from your graves, O my people. And l will put my Spirit within you, and you shall live, and I will place you in your own land. Then you shall know that I am the LORD; I have spoken, and I will do it, declares the LORD,' "(Ezekiel 37:11-14).** The world is big, yes. But God is bigger...Your world is tiny, yes. But God gets tinier. Not one dust mite falls through the carpet fibers and into the pad apart from your Father. He's big enough that small doesn't matter...Understand this: we are both tiny and massive. We are nothing more than molded clay given breath, but we are nothing less than divine self-portraits, huffing and puffing along mountain ranges of epic narrative arcs prepared for us by the Infinite Word Himself...You are as spoken by God as stars. The God who breathed air into your lungs in the beginning sees you still. He knows. And He cares about all of it and He cares about all of you.

The devil is a liar and brings condemnation; he is the accuser of the brethren. In Christ we've been *set free* **(See Romans 8:1-2).**

God gives grace freely to people who don't deserve it. **"You see, at just the right time, when we were still powerless, Christ died for the ungodly. Very rarely will anyone die for a righteous person, though for a good person someone might possibly dare to die, But God demonstrates his own love for us in this: while we were still sinners, Christ died for us,"(Romans 5:6-11).** But without faith it's impossible to please God. The way to be delivered from self is to be occupied by Christ.

**"Do not conform to the pattern of this world, but be transformed by the renewing of your mind. Then you will be able to test and approve what God's will is- his good, pleasing and perfect will." (Romans 12:2)**

Did you grow up fearful, insecure, never measuring up, never hearing words of affirmation and approval? What's the source of your anxiety, what feeds your worries? Until you express your fears you can't expel them. You must fight hard to shine the light of words upon it. If your fear becomes a wordless darkness that you avoid, perhaps even manage to forget, you open yourself to further attacks of fear.

I thank God that in His gracious plan to bless and use me, He has allowed me to go through hard times, through trials that many people go through. God is good at reaching down and making something beautiful out of even the worst situations. When the rape scene reappeared, I knew that the Holy Spirit was prompting me to trust God's love, His power, His sufficiency and ability to overrule, and His transforming presence within me. It

*Beauty for Ashes*

was time, time for me to let go of the past and let God set me free, to truly forgive through His grace. I praise the Lord that I need not strive toward a possible victory but can live from a position of victory already won. Although we live in the world our weapons are not against flesh and blood, we do not fight against mankind, so to speak. **"The weapons we fight with are not the weapons of the world. On the contrary, they have divine power to demolish strongholds. We demolish arguments and every pretension that sets itself against the knowledge of God, and we take captive every thought to make it obedient to Christ."** (2 Cor.10.4-5)

***Jesus said that those who love Him will keep his commands (John.14:15-21).*** The enemy has launched malicious disinformation campaigns that have effectively enslaved many people for years to low self-esteem, self-hatred, guilt, eating disorders, perversions, inordinate fears, and all kinds of destructive habits and addictions, and some things that have been out of your control.

**"What then shall we say to these things? If God be for us who can be against us? He who did not spare His only Son, but gave him up for us all – how will he not also, along with him, graciously give us all things? Who will bring any charge against those whom God has chosen? It is God who justifies. Who then is the one who condemns? No one. Christ Jesus who died-more than that, who was raised to life-is at the right hand of God and is also interceding for us. Who shall separate us from the love of Christ? Shall trouble or hardship or persecution or famine or nakedness or danger or sword? As it is written: "For your sake we face death all day long; we are considered as sheep to be slaughtered." No, in all these things we are more than conquerors through him who loved us. For I am convinced that neither death nor life, neither angels nor demons, neither the present nor the future, nor any powers, neither height nor depth, nor anything else in creation, will be able to separate us from the love of God that is in Christ Jesus our Lord. (Romans 8:31-39)**

When we humans exercise our freedom, we act in our own self-interest, putting the needs of others far behind our own and endeavor to solve our own problems whenever they occur. Disaster results. The problem is, the extent to which we believe in our freedom is the extent to which we will never acknowledge our need for a Savior.

Author Tullian Tchividjian says: "While it is gloriously true for the Christian that there is nowhere Christ has not arrived by His Spirit, there is a converse and more sobering truth: there is no part of any Christian in this life that is free of sin. Because of the totality of sin's effect, therefore, we never outgrow our need for Christ's finished work on our behalf. We never graduate beyond our desperate need for Christ's righteousness."

The reason this is so important is because we will always be suspicious of grace until we realize our desperate need for it. Our dire need for God's grace doesn't get smaller after God saves us; it actually gets bigger. Christian growth is always growth into grace, not away from it. Because of human nature, you and I were desperate for God's grace before we were saved. Because of human nature, you and I remain desperate for God's grace even after we are saved.

## Remaining Sin

"I do not understand what I do. For what I do want to do I do not do, but what I hate I do,"(Romans 7:15). Paul, like us, has been raised from the dead and is now alive to Christ, but remaining sin continues to plague him at every level and in every way.

Jesus, however, didn't come for the free. He came to proclaim release to the captives. We aren't free to choose Jesus; He chooses us. This is Good News! **"You did not choose me, but I chose you and appointed you so that you might go and bear fruit—fruit that will last- and so that whatever you ask in my name the Father will give you," (John 15:18).** This is the Good News. We desperately need the goodness of God's sovereignty precisely because of the bondage of our free will.

The system that overrides us is a gracious one. As we run from God, as we rebel, and as we exert our free will, God leaves the ninety-nine sheep who do not need rescuing to come find us-the lost ones-and gathers us up in His arms and carries us home.

# CHAPTER FIVE

## His Everlasting Love

Have you ever wondered why you have such a tender heart towards God, but life is just not working for you? You have not experienced the abundant life Christ died to give you here on Earth. **"My son, do not let wisdom and understanding out of your sight, preserve sound judgement and discretion; they will be life for you, an ornament to grace your neck. Then you will go on your way in safety, and your foot will not stumble. When you lie down you will not be afraid; when you lie down, your sleep will be sweet. Have no fear of sudden disaster or of the ruin that overtakes the wicked, for the LORD will be at your side and will keep your foot from being snared."(Proverb 3:21-26)**

Believers in Christ never ever face adversity alone, the LORD has promised never to leave us nor forsake us. **"Never will I leave you: never will I forsake you."(Hebrews 13:5a)** Many Christians think that God is perpetually disappointed with them. But because of what Jesus did for us on the Cross, God sees us as friends and children, not as enemies and strangers. God is a good Father, and because we're with Jesus, God's affection for us is unchanging and His approval of us is forever.

But of course, we forget, among us, who knows all our violations, or has felt sufficient remorse for things we do wrong? If the cleansing of our confession depends on the confessor, we are all sunk, for none of us have confessed adequately or accurately. Isaiah says; **"All of us have become like one who is unclean and our righteous acts are like filthy rags."** (Isaiah 64:6)

Stop being mad at yourself because you're still struggling in certain areas. When it comes to an area of your life that needs improvement, be concerned about it, but not consumed with it. You are always going to be working on something, so learn to separate you "who" from your "do." Who you are in Christ is a settled issue. **"There is therefore now no condemnation to those who are in Christ Jesus" (Romans 8:1 NKJV).** Because God has chosen to see you "in Christ," you are always acceptable to Him and you always have access to Him. We condemn ourselves! God will convict us, and when we repent of sin, He will cleanse us, but He will never condemn us. Satan does that. But God never will. **"Who is he who condemns? It is Christ who died, and furthermore is also risen, who is even at the right hand of God, who makes intercession for us." (Romans 8:34 NKJV)**

Every time you fail, Christ your advocate offers His atoning blood to cover your sin. As a result, God sees you as "accepted." Stop comparing yourself to somebody else. You are you, and you will never be them. We are all equal in Christ! So, when somebody condemns you, stand on this Scripture: **"Surely the Lord God will help Me; who is he who will condemn Me? Indeed they will all grow old like a garment; the moth will eat them up." (Isaiah 50:9 NKJV)**

# CHAPTER SIX

# In Prison

I tossed and turned gently trying so hard not to wake up my bed-banker. Being imprisoned was hitting home pretty quickly, the seriousness of my situation began to get the better of me. Life without my immediate family members? My grandson, my daughter and of course my son were soon becoming a reality I needed to come to terms with. With no way of affording an immigration lawyer, all stakes seemed to be working against me. But the LORD hears the cry of His afflicted. In spite of what I think or feel when l get my eyes off the LORD, I'm learning not to resist my trials as intruders, but to welcome them as friends, knowing that God uses each difficulty and my momentary troubles to humble me and perfect my faith. The Lord uses all the bad and the good in our lives to produce in us the quality of endurance and new growth in godliness that He longs to see in His children, for an eternal glory that far outweighs our troubled lives.

**"Blessed is the one you discipline, LORD the one you teach from your law; you grant them relief from days of trouble, till a pit is dug for the wicked. For the LORD will not reject his people; he will never forsake his inheritance: "(Psalms 94:12-14).**

**Only you can make you Bitter, No One Else Can**

You can be angry and choose to forgive, no one can make you bitter but yourself. While we are always tempted to constantly locate our identity in something or someone smaller than Jesus, the Gospel liberates us by revealing that our true identity is locked in Christ. Our connection in and with Christ is the truest definition of who we are. Those of us who have done parenting and those with young ones know that, much of their learning involves a lot of reminding our children of who they are in Christ, what they already possess in Christ, and how nothing—nothing—that Christ has secured for them or any believers can ever be taken away.

People and circumstances don't determine your attitude, you do! To win in life you must learn to focus on your opportunities, not your rights. Paul wrote from a prison cell: **"Whatever is true, whatever is noble, whatever is right, whatever is pure, whatever is lovely, whatever is admirable if anything is excellent or praise worthy think about such things,"(See Phil. 4:8).** By no means am I comparing myself with Paul, and neither was I imprisoned for the same reasons, my reasons for being in prison were consequences for my own wrong-doing. I've quoted this verse to show my assumed state of mind when I was in prison.

Although, circumstances could lock Paul in, they couldn't keep him down. One of our biggest causes of discontent is our constant struggle to secure our right. Sometimes we feel we've been wronged, or we haven't gotten a fair shake. That's because we live in an imperfect world. And as long as we do, we will not see a time when everything we do is justly rewarded. So, we are faced with a decision. Are you going to spend your time on what should have been, or get over it and focus on what can be? Even when truth and justice are on your side, you may never be able to right all wrongs. But ultimately God will, so leave it in His hands. When fighting for our rights becomes our mode of thinking, "fighting for your rights" fuels in your emotions of resentment and anger, because these destructive emotions sap your energy and make you negative.

When you focus on your rights, you are usually looking backward. You can't make progress when you are facing the wrong way! Only when you focus in the right direction will you move in the right direction. Now this doesn't mean you won't experience pain; it just means you choose to forgive, and zero in on what you can control--your attitude and opportunities. We live in an imperfect world. All our imperfections are swallowed up by God's perfect love. We may have made mistakes, but it's never too late to receive His forgiveness and receive courage and strength from Him to do the right thing. **"What then? Shall we sin because we are not under the law but under grace? By no** means! Don't you know that when you offer yourselves to someone as obedient slaves, you are slaves to the one you obey – whether you are slaves to sin, which leads to death, or to obedience, which leads to righteousness? But thanks be to God that, though you used to be slaves to sin, you have come to obey from the heart the pattern of teaching that has now claimed your allegiance. You have been set free from sin and have become slaves to righteousness,"(Romans 6:15-18).** As creatures who regularly fail, our nature is sinful, and we are in a continual struggle for the integrity of our soul. We look to God for strength in the face of temptation and for forgiveness from our sin. A heart seeking to *live* in God ascends along a narrow and difficult path by foregoing the world and its traps and vices. This transformation happens by degrees.

However, if we give in to a "rationalizing" faith, we may find ourselves hanging on to sin and losing our progression in one, true direction toward our God. If we rationalize sin in any area of our life, we are trying to "manage" it rather than surrender it to God. For example, we may be capable of recognizing our own sinful nature, as well as admitting that it is hateful to God, while continuing to preserve a proud attitude, hardened to the reality that "the body is dead because of sin" (Romans 8:10) as long as we fail to abandon ourselves completely to God, maintaining some part of ourselves separated from God and free to indulge as we desire, we will remain spiritually blind.

But when in wrenching remorse we seek the Lord's love and complete forgiveness, in returning wholly to the Lord, opening all areas of our lives to His light, Satan and his shadows are swept out of each corner, in all areas, and ultimately, we find the release and relief of God's forgiveness. All of us are given the chance for this same kind of transformation, which occurs through receiving God's forgiveness of our sins in thought and action-totally.

You must believe what God says about you, over what everyone else says. Stop listening to those who claim you'll never amount to anything. You might've had a bad childhood, a failed marriage, or career, or life has just been hard on you. **"Forgetting**

**those things which are behind, and reaching forth unto those things which are ahead [of you]." (Phil 3:13)**

The Bible doesn't say that *we* call those things which are not as though they are. Nor does it say *others* have the power to speak things which are not as though they are over your life. No, it is ***God***, through His Word, Who speaks into existence His will for your life. That is the best news! Our responsibility is to line up our will with God's will. When we do, He empowers us to accomplish what normally would be humanly impossible. The Bible says, **"The just shall live by faith," (Romans 1:17).** Your faith is more important than your performance. Yes, when God decrees something, we get to participate in it. But in every case, it's God who ***performs*** it. The thing you are worried about performing, God says will be done through ***His*** power. Will you experience delays and disappointments? Yes, but ultimately you won't be denied, for God has decreed it. **"All things work together for good to those who love God, to those who are the called according to his purpose," (Romans 8:28NKJV).**

## My Journal Continues

No matter which way I sliced it, it seemed like, my family was going to reap the repercussions of an absentee parent, that's never something any parent wants to see happen to their family. Yes, my children were fairly mature now, but God never intends that family separate, not in this manner anyway. The unit of family is way too important to God, that's why it's number one target on the devil's long list to destroy God's people. Satan will do anything and everything to separate and destroy the family unit. I had thought by paying all my fines and costs the past would go away, but now all I needed to understand is, why had God allowed this? What lesson was He teaching me? I had to ask the LORD what all these meant…what His plan and purpose for me is?

That's what the battle in your life is about. The Holy Spirit, Who is your Teacher: wants you to search God's Word for answers and direction. **(See John 16:15 NIV)** He doesn't want you to be passive and simply accept whatever comes into your life. The Scripture teaches us that God wants you and I to turn to His Word for insight; to find divine solutions to the human problems confronting you and me, day in and day out, even our mistakes. He wants us to stand on His Word instead of lying down and saying, "I guess this is just the way it's got to be." Your Bible is a road map that will never steer you the wrong way. It's a sword you can fight with and win every time. **"For the word of God** *is* **quick, and powerful, and sharper than any two-edged sword, piercing even to the dividing asunder of soul and spirit, and of the joints and marrow, and** *is* **a discerner of the thoughts and intents of the heart," (Hebrews 4:12 NKJV).**

During trials, the LORD will show you who your true friends are. God has a way of opening our eyes even when we don't want to see signs of betrayal. This includes letting go of friends or loved ones that have been in our lives since we could remember, but do not mean well for the life and purpose God has for us to live to His glory. When real trouble knocks on your door, God allows you to see people for who they really are. Those you thought and for sure expected to be in your corner are nowhere to be seen, or worse, they are the very ones talking behind your back. This never happens without God having given us warnings here and there that we choose to overlook, at least I did.

When we ignore these signs, we will suffer at the hands of those very people, and, or get hurt. Don't hang onto things too tightly when the Lord is showing you signs and reasons why you need to distance yourself from some people who were only meant to be in your life for a season. God knows best, sooner or later you will realize why they had to leave your life. Not everyone belongs in your God ordained destiny. **"The LORD confides in those who fear him; he makes his covenant known to them. My eyes are ever on the LORD, for only he will release my feet from the snare. Turn to me and be gracious to me, for I am lonely and afflicted. Relieve the troubles of my heart and free me from my anguish. Look on my affliction and my distress and take away all my sins. See how numerous are my enemies and how fiercely they hate me!"(Psalm 25:14-19)**

So now whose report was I going to believe? Was I going to be overcome by my circumstances, or was I going to believe what the Lord says in His Word, that He will not allow me to go through that which am not able to handle. The Law, says Paul in Galatians 3, served as a taskmaster until Christ came. In other words, the Law functions to drive us to Christ, to our need for a Savior. Of course, now that Christ has come, Paul says that we are no longer under a taskmaster. We are now under the tutelage of a gracious Father who, even when He disciplines us, is loving us unconditionally all the way home!

"Sin is the primary condition of humanity's fallen nature and nothing blinds us and separates us from the Lord as effectively as our sin. The most earnest heart seeking communion with God, is also desperately human and, therefore, prone to sin. Even as born-again believers in a progression toward God, this inborn tendency to "forget" God through transgression will keep us fluctuating between moments of true ecstatic faith and the pull of our eyes to focus on the world and its lies. Because of the power of sin to blind us to spiritual reality, when we do sin, we are often blind to the fact of our sin." (***Spiritually Blind*** by James P. Gills, M.D.)

For that reason, we are truly dependent on the working of the Holy Spirit to bring conviction to our hearts, showing us the true nature of our sin through the Word of God. Only as we choose to recognize and confess our sin can we have our spiritual eyes opened, so that through repentance of our sin we can be cleansed and set free.

Like in the parable of the Good Samaritan (See Luke 10:25-37). Instead of telling this parable to help us learn a moralistic lesson about being nice to people, Jesus is showing us how far from being like the Good Samaritan - and how much like the priest and Levite - we actually are, Jesus' parable aims to destroy our efforts to justify ourselves, to find a class of people we can call neighbors that we actually do love. We move from being identified with the priest and the Levite - to never perfectly loving our best friends as ourselves, much less our enemies, to being identified with the traveler in desperate need of salvation.

Jesus intends the parable itself to leave us beaten and bloodied, lying in a ditch, like the man in the story. We are the needy, unable to do anything to help ourselves. We are the broken, beaten up by life, robbed of hope. ***But then Jesus comes.*** Casting the Samaritan - considered an enemy by the average Jew - as the hero of the story is a reminder that Jesus has identified with those far from God to bring them near, that He has "become sin" to cancel sin's debt.

Unlike the priest and Levite, Jesus doesn't avoid us. He crosses over the street, from Heaven to Earth, comes into our mess, and gets His hands dirty. At great cost to Himself on the Cross, He heals our wounds, covers our nakedness, and loves us with a no-strings-attached love. He brings us to the Father and promises that His help is simply not a onetime gift - rather, it's a gift that will forever cover future charges we incur. Jesus is the Good Samaritan.

## You Have Been Here Long Enough

I was too wrapped up in my momentary troubles, weaknesses, needs, self-centeredness and (especially my self-reliance and pride), the loss of both my brother and father had taken me to a place I barely recognized. There were also other unfathomable wrongs that brought deep hurt and scarred close loved ones. This was an extremely dark place for me; I backslid and became self-destructive. In distress and wounded, I became a bitter and resentful person, with a chip on my shoulder...the world owed me something. The afflicted man in Psalm 102 prayed with loud groaning. **"My heart is blighted and withered like grass...I am like a desert owl, like an owl among the ruins."** If we have deep troubles. God tells us to pour out our hearts to Him. (Psalm 62:8) Leaving our feelings in God's hands helps us to be more consistent in prayer. And we're not to let our emotions determine whether or not to pray. And if the Spirit carries us along in prayer, let's be grateful. But if not, we can still pray in faith based on God's Word. **"I am coming to you now, but I say these things**

**while I am still in the world, so that they may have the full measure of my joy within them. I have given them your word and the world has hated them, for they are not of the world any more than I am of the world. My prayer is not that you take them out of the world but that you protect them from the evil one. They are not of the world, even as I am not of it. Sanctify them by the truth; your word of truth. As you sent me into the world, I have sent them into the world. For them I sanctify myself, that they too may be sanctified." (John 17:13-19)**

To endure the harsh treatment of life and not be controlled by these conditions, and not to return anger for anger, or evil for evil, reminds me of the humility and courage that a grace-captured heart can have. When God opens your spiritual eyes and you can admit that you too have made mistakes, then only are you able to ask yourself, who am I to hold a grudge? With God nothing is incidental, and no experience is wasted; every trial that He allows to happen is a platform on which He reveals Himself, showing His love and power, both to me and to others looking on. For God holds our future and He always will, now and forever. His power to heal from the inside out is unlimited. His ability is absolute and beyond imagining when we put our total trust in Him, then only can a heart be set free in some way. And only the Gospel can truly set a heart free.

When we cling to the attitude that we belong to ourselves rather than to the Lord, we are seeking an independence from our Creator, rather than the dependence upon Him that He wants from us. We are owned by Him through our redemption because we have been bought with a price - the blood of His Son, Jesus Christ. Through salvation, we are freed from our self-ownership that has only served to cause us worry, the fear of loss, envy and covetousness, among other sins.

Our continued trust in ourselves, and our own refusal to release our lives fully into God's hands prevents us from living the abundant life Christ died for us to live. Only as we abandon ourselves to God can we experience the wonderful freedom the Apostle Paul enjoyed, as he declared, **"It is no longer I who live, but Christ lives in me," (Galatians 2:20).** The beautiful, loving character of Christ will be displayed in all of our thoughts, motives, and actions. Only in that way can we **"...be filled with all the fullness of God," (Ephesians 3:19).** The thief, the devil only comes to destroy, discourage and stop or hinder us from living and enjoying the promises and blessings of the abundant life that Christ died for us to live, to experience our individual God ordained destiny. (See John 10:10)

No matter what we have been through in life, the mistakes, misfortunes, prolonged illnesses, loss of a loved one, or our own self destructive lifestyles we pick up along life's journey, and defeating circumstances we often find ourselves in…God's not up there scratching His head wondering what to do next. He says in His word; **"No weapon that is formed against thee shall prosper; and every tongue *that* shall rise against thee in judgement thou shalt condemn. This *is* the heritage of the servants of the LORD, and their righteousness *is* of me, saith the LORD," (Isaiah 54:17).** God created us to leave our marks on our generation. You have a God ordained purpose to fulfill, you are still here for a reason. One word from God will course correct your life! He's waiting for you to call upon Him. **"So shall my word be that goeth out of my mouth: it shall not return unto me void, but it shall accomplish that which I please, and it shall prosper in the thing whereto I sent it," (Isaiah 55:11).**The mess you've made God already knew you would, and yet He chose you in Christ before the foundation of the world, anyway! Think about that. You may feel like you've fallen behind. Maybe you are not where you hoped to be in life. You have big dreams in your heart, but you haven't caught any good breaks. Doors have closed. It's easy to get discouraged. But my challenge for you is: if you will keep being your best day in and day out, if you will live a life that honors God, He will not only make up for lost time, He will thrust you further. He will do more than you can even ask or think.

In the Bible we read about David's victory against Goliath. He didn't have any military training. All the odds were against him, but he knew the Most High God was with him. When David defeated Goliath in a split second, he became a national hero. One touch of God's favor thrust him many, many years ahead. What's interesting is God used an obstacle to promote David. When you face giant obstacles in your own life---disappointments, setbacks, things don't work out---don't become discouraged. That adversity could be the very thing God will use to promote you. **"But God demonstrates his own love for us in this: While we were still sinners, Christ died for us," (Romans 5:8).** He's the Creator of everything, and nothing we do surprises Him. God sees and knows the end from the beginning. **"For you created my inmost being; you knit me together in my mother's womb. I praise you because I am fearfully and wonderfully made; your works are wonderful, I know that full well. My frame was not hidden from you when I was made in the secret place, when I was woven together in the depth of the earth. Your eyes saw my unformed body; all the days ordained for me were written in your book before one of them came to be. How precious to me are your thoughts, God!" (Psalms 139:13-17).** The God who created you has a plan for your life; you have considered your difficult circumstances long enough. You've considered the medical report, the bank statement, and the odds against them over and over. It's okay to acknowledge the facts, but you don't have to dwell on them. There is another report, God's report. Now is time to make a switch and start considering God, who created you and knows the plans He has for you anyway. God's report says, **"Because he loves me," says the Lord, "I will rescue him, I will protect him, for he acknowledges my name. He will call on me, and I will answer him; I will be with him in trouble, I will deliver him and honor him. With long life I will satisfy him and show him my salvation," (Psalm 91: 14-16).** The Word of God reveals to you His blessings for you in salvation through His Son Jesus Christ, and with the help of Christ who gives you strength and power, you are able then to say: **"I know what it is to be in need, and I know what it is to have plenty. I have learned the secret of being content in any and every situation, whether well fed or hungry, whether living in plenty or in want. I can do all things through him who gives me strength," (Philippians 4: 12-13).**

Nobody was ever born without talent, including you, but you have to find it. Paul writes, **"There are diversities of gifts, but the same Spirit."** What kind of company are you keeping?

The old saying goes, "Birds of the same feathers flock together." Aristotle said, *"We are what we repeatedly do. Excellence then is not an act, but a habit."* If you run around with turkeys, you'll never fly with eagles." God is not only the giver of your gift; He supplies the strength to function successfully in it. The Scripture says, **"He who walks with wise men, will be wise," (Pr. 13:20 NKJV).** Therefore, the company we keep, failing to spend time in prayer and God's Word keeps us from discovering and developing our God given unique gifts. So, if you want to succeed, consult God, and operate in your God given strength.

Author Paula White writes: "The Christian's self-esteem is ultimately that person's individual judgement about their worthiness in Christ. Your reputation lies in the truth that you have been saved and belong to God, that you have been equipped in Christ to face any situation of life and overcome it, and that you are lovable because Christ first loved you. You're forgiven of all past sins and you are not a product of your past. You are capable of walking in newness of life because the Holy Spirit has promised to be with you constantly as your guide, Comforter and Teacher."

God is God, and there is no one like Him. Nothing is beyond His influence or control. There is no sin He can't forgive if the person is willing to be forgiven. There is no relationship He cannot mend if both people are willing to come into alignment with His principles. There is no obstacle that He cannot remove, change or overcome. Did you know that you have access to the generational blessing of a family in Christ? Did you know that you have been given an identity in Christ that is astounding? Was there a message growing up that validated or contradicted the message that God has for you in His Word? Discover by reading and studying God's Word, it's His letter to you and me. These various traits that the Bible identifies as our identity in Christ are true for every person who accepts Jesus Christ as their Savior. ***Salvation is key!*** *Anything that is not Christ-centered is a dead work.*

# CHAPTER SEVEN

## God Is Your Answer

In Prison: Being in complete compliance with my fines and cost due to the State, I had put my past to rest. But my momentary poor judgement and choice was about to turn my life upside down. Yes, my dues to the State were settled. Now I was under judgement to the immigration law. To my dismay and horror, I realized I was facing deportation.

Contrary to popular belief, Christianity is not about good people getting better. If anything, it is about bad people coping with their failure to be good. That is to say, Christianity concerns the Gospel, which is nothing more or less than the Good News that, **"...Christ Jesus came into the world to save sinners...," (1 Timothy 1:15).**

Sited among the hurting, the defeated, the bitter, the angry, the depressed and the hopeless, the "outcasts", the poor, the sick, the lame, the bereaved, whatever it is that has come to bend you over, like the story in the Scriptures about the woman with the issue of blood ...Christ is calling each one of us, saying you've been here for a long time, you were never meant to camp here. Refuse to be overcome by your situation, the arm of flesh will fail you, instead be overcome by the blood of Jesus Christ. Turn to Gods' open arms, through Christ His Son you have already been rescued, all you need to do is to answer that call from Jesus and acknowledge Him as your Savior!

**"Here a great number of disabled people used to lie- the blind, the lame, and the paralyzed. One who was there had been an invalid for thirty-eight years. When he saw him lying there and learned that he had been in this condition for a long time, he asked him, do you want to get well?" "Sir," the invalid replied, "I have no one to help me into the pool when the water**

*Jacqueline Fusallah*

is stirred. While I am trying to get in, someone else goes down ahead before me." Then Jesus said to him, "Get up! Pick up your mat and walk." At once the man was cured; he picked up his mat and walked." The day on which this took place was a Sabbath, and so the Jewish leaders said to the man who had been healed, "It is the Sabbath; the law forbids you to carry your mat." But he replied, "The man who made me well said to me, "Pick up your mat and walk."" So they asked him, "Who is this fellow who told you to pick up your mat and walk?" The man who had been healed had no idea who it was, for Jesus had slipped away into the crowd that was there. Later Jesus found him at the temple and said to him, "See, you are well again. Stop sinning or something worse may happen to you." The man went away and told the Jewish leaders that it was Jesus who had made him well. (John 5:3-14 NIV)

Jesus has something to give you… "Will you be made whole? It is time to leave our past behind, put the past in His hands and be made whole. Jesus is calling to you… "Will you pick up your mat and walk?" We have to make our mind up to pick up our trails, our pain, failures, our painful past, the abuse, the betrayals, the mistakes and our poor judgement…it's time to forgive yourself and others, and it's time to answer the call from Jesus, "Will you be made whole?" It is time to pick up your mat and walk! It's time to turn your stumbling block into a stepping stone in the name of Jesus. Heap all of your burdens and lay them at the Cross, when you believe Christ makes you whole, receive it, believe it, declare it and in the Mighty name of Jesus it is established!

Author Tullian Tchividjian says, "There is an all-important distinction Christians must make between horizontal consequences of sin and vertical condemnation for sin. When a Christian falls into sin, lots of people confuse these two categories, which results in two basic responses. Some people question their friend's salvation: 'How could anybody really be a Christian and do something like that?' Others say, 'Just let it go. After all, nobody is perfect. Don't we believe in grace and forgiveness?' "

The first group needs to be reminded that God's love for you, and acceptance of us does not in any way depend on what we do or don't do, but rather on what Jesus has done. Who we are before God is firmly anchored in Jesus' accomplishment, not ours.

The second group needs to be reminded that consequences on the ground of life are real. Real people make real mistakes that require real action to be taken. So, for instance, we can talk bad about our boss without sacrificing one ounce of God's acceptance, because before God, our sin has been atoned for, our guilt has been removed **(Isa.6:7)**. But we might still lose our job. We can make the mistake of driving one hundred miles per hour without losing a bit of God's love for us, because nothing can separate us from the love of God in Christ Jesus. But we might still lose our license.

When we confuse consequences with condemnation and vice versa, we don't know how to make sense of things when our brother or sister makes a big mistake.

The truth is that when we are in the throes of consequences for foolish things we do, our only hope is to remember that **"...there is therefore now no condemnation for those who are in Christ Jesus," (Rom.8:1 ESV)**. In fact, the kind of suffering that comes from the consequences of sin is like a brushfire that burns away every thread of hope we have in ourselves and leaves only the thread of divine grace- a thread that will never break no matter how foolish we may be. Today, know that Jesus knows your ordeal and your pain. And know that He promises to never leave you nor forsake you. Jesus came for, and rescues, broken people, because broken people are all that there are.

**What, or Who You focus on, is everything.**

**"Very truly I tell you, unless a kernel of wheat falls to the ground and dies, it remains only a single seed. But if it dies, it produces many seeds. Anyone who loves their life will lose it, while anyone who hates their life in this world will keep it for eternal life. Whoever serves me must follow me; and where I am, my servant also will be. My father will honor the one who serves me. (John 12:24-26)**

The five years I had been out of work was the most beneficial time spent in the Lord's presence and His Word. When the Lord began to reveal to me the danger of my own thoughts. I began to purposely and consistently devote my time reading God's Word and praying. This changed my thinking and my living. When you speak what God speaks over your life, you change, and then you change your circumstances.

When you submit your thoughts to God's Spirit, allowing Him to approve or renew or replace them with His thoughts, anxiety and depression cannot continue to control you. Avoid those who speak discouraging words and hang out with those who speak **"...a good word" [that] makes [your heart] glad," (Proverbs 12:25NAS).** This is not always possible if in fact family plays a role. With prayer and total trust in what God can do is vital, the battle is the Lords. **"For with God nothing shall be impossible," (Luke 1:37).**

I thank God for His wisdom in allowing the things that have influenced me throughout my life-the things that have prepared my heart to respond to Him and to live for His glory, and to experience His everlasting love. God still loves us even when we sin! And how much we also need to let God's love flow out to others, as we experience His love and grace. I thank the Lord that life's struggles persuade me to seek the secret place. They remind me for my need for a Savior. May God's Spirit fill us day-by-day, bringing forth the fresh, abundant fruit of love in our lives. Love that keeps growing richer in knowledge and wise insight, in patience and kindness, in humility that honors the other person. Love that overcomes jealousy and arrogance and self-seeking. Love that is not touchy or resentful. Love that covers a multitude of sins and refuses to gossip. Love that chooses to look out for the other person's interests, as well as our own-whether we feel like it or not. May God work in us this kind of love - and especially for those we find hard to love and those who rub us the wrong way. May the world see God's love in our lives, and may many be drawn to Christ.

Every so often, I let my momentary troubles to remind me when I first invited Christ into my heart. Years ago when I let go

*Beauty for Ashes*

of the whole burden of my sins and rested on the atoning work of Christ - on the total payment He made for me on the Cross…I thank God for that today, in that same simple way, I can let go of the whole burden of my life …my children, and all my past, present and future relationships, my self-dependence and my inadequacies, and rest on His presence working in me through the Holy Spirit, when by grace I live like this, then I've lived a fulfilled peaceful day.

God's still working on all of us as long as we remain in these fleshly bodies. Salvation is a continuance work by the Holy Spirit. But my confidence is in His Word; **"Being confident of this one thing, that he which hath begun a good work in you will perform** *it* **until the day of Jesus Christ:" (Philippians 1:6).** I would never have imagined that one could experience such peace while in prison. But I did. (Isaiah 26:3)

Your answer is found in receiving a fresh revelation of just how much you are forgiven in Christ and believing that you are no longer under condemnation. The Scriptures says; **"Bless the LORD, O my soul; and all that is within me, bless His holy name! Bless the LORD, O my soul, and forget not all His benefits: Who forgives all your iniquities, who heals all your diseases," (Psalm. 103:1-3).** Now which comes first? The consciousness that all your sins are forgiven precedes the healing of all your diseases!

And the operative word here is *all*. Some of us are comfortable with receiving partial forgiveness in certain areas of our lives. But we refuse to allow Jesus' forgiveness to touch some dark areas - areas that we can't let go of and that we can't forgive ourselves for, or others. Whatever those mistakes maybe, I encourage you to allow Jesus to forgive you of *all* your sins and receive healing for *all* your diseases. Let the past go. Let the mistakes go. Allow yourself to be free and learn to forgive yourself by receiving with an open heart Jesus' total and complete forgiveness.

When I began to focus on Christ's forgiveness of all my sins instead of myself, I was able to encourage others in prison, l was able to share the Gospel with them. The Bible says, **"Faith is** the substance of things hoped for," (Heb.11:1). You don't need faith unless you're hoping for something. Hope establishes the goal; faith is the bridge that establishes it. There's no need of building a bridge if you're not going anywhere. But if you're going after something you can't reach on your own, you need the bridge of faith to get you there. **"This is the victory that overcometh the world, even our faith," (1 John 5:4).** Unless people learn to stand in faith in God's Word, they'll end up using willpower and discipline to fight the Devil, and they'll lose. Jesus told Peter, **"I have prayed for you, that your faith should not fail," (Luke 22:32 NKJV).**

When you're up to your neck in problems and don't know which way to turn, speak to yourself and say, "Faith don't fail me now!" The Bible says, **"Faith cometh by hearing and hearing by the word of God," (Romans 10:17).** It's in hearing yourself declare God's Word that your faith grows. Another Scripture says; **"But the word which they heard did not profit them, not being mixed with faith in those who heard it," (Heb.4:2).** You can have the *expression* of faith, yet not enjoy the *benefits* of faith. You can get excited about a sermon in Church, yet nothing changes in your life. You've got to get the "mix" right. You've got to get what you *hear* and mix it with what you *think, say* and *do*. Faith is not an emotion; it's a decision to stand on God's Word.

What you focus on is so important. What are you dwelling on right now? Is it the size of the obstacle, or the size of your God? If you go around all day long thinking about your problems, worried, anxious, and playing all the negative scenarios in your mind, you will draw in the negative.

You're using your faith but you're using it in the reverse. It takes the same amount of energy to be negative as it takes to be positive. It also takes the same amount of energy to worry as it does to believe, use your energy for the right purposes. And that is how, right in prison I used my energy thanking God in advance for working in my favor, I thanked Him for the answers on the way. With every breath in me I prayed: "Lord, Thank You that You are still on the throne. You have me in the palm of Your hand, and nothing can snatch me away."

When you make God bigger, your problems become smaller. When you magnify God instead of magnifying your difficulties, faith rises in your heart. That faith will keep you fully persuaded. Pay attention to what you focus on. Be aware of what's playing in your mind all day. Are you considering your circumstances, or are you considering your God? Your present situation is a fact, but God's Word is truth. **"For the word of the LORD is right and true; he is faithful in all he does," (Psalm 33: 4).**

One time Jesus was on His way to pray for a sick girl in a nearby town. Along the way He was stopped time and again, one delay after another. At one point these people came up and said to those with Jesus, **"Tell Jesus He doesn't need to come any more. It's too late. She's dead."**

The Scripture says Jesus overheard it but ignored it. Sometimes in order to stay in faith you have to ignore a negative report. It doesn't mean you ignore the facts and act like they are not there. Instead, just like Jesus, you may hear the negative report, but you choose not to dwell on it. Many inmates made a big joke of my faith, and especially when they realized that "all my eggs" were held in the balance of me representing myself before the judge in my own case wholly trusting in God's favor. And that, did not sit well with many inmates, they mocked me, some thought I was being arrogant or simply ignorant. I don't recommend what I did to anyone unless you have heard from the Lord and you are confident with your case.

If you are to have unshakable faith and become everything God created you to be, then learn to ignore the negative report and choose to believe the report of the Lord. It is important to know facts, but it's most important to step out of the natural and say, *"This may be impossible with man, but I know with God all things are possible."* Make sure you don't talk yourself out of what God wants to do in your life. It may not seem logical. All your reasoning may say it will never happen. You may feel you are too old, or you don't have the experience. It may seem that the report is too bad, and all the odds are against you.

I'm not telling you someone else's story, I am telling you my own life experiences, my journey with God through the mistakes I've made, or the mistakes others have made that have affected me. Through all these there are lessons to be learnt if your desire is to grow in God. Beware of trusting in yourself—which is not wise. Instead, walk in wisdom and you will be kept safe. The essence of wisdom is to trust in God more than yourself or other people. The Spirit of God will guide you with counsel, so take all your concerns to Him. When you feel confused, it may be helpful to write out your prayer, asking Him to show you the way forward. Then wait in His Presence, giving Him time to guide your mind while you focus on Him and His Word. Always praying in the name of Jesus. Call on the name "Jesus," to help you stay focused. "The name of the LORD is a strong tower, the righteous run to it and are safe." (Proverbs 18:10)

We may not understand how something can happen, but we don't reason it out. We don't come up with excuses. We do as Abraham did and become fully persuaded. You may be sick, but God puts the promise in your heart that He will restore your health unto you. You can say, "The doctor's report doesn't look good. My great-grandmother died of this same thing. It's been in our family for five generations." You can talk yourself out of believing the best, or you can stand on God's promises and believe Him!

The Bible says, **"God's word will not return unto Him void, but it shall accomplish that which He pleases, and it shall prosper in the thing whereto He sent it. (See Isaiah 55:7-11)** . You don't need your boss to give you a promotion. You don't need someone with power to help you catch a break. God's promises are not dependent on who you know or who you don't know. The main thing is for you to know *Him*, stand on His *Word* and *believe* it. Sometimes the word "no" simply means "not now" but ask again." So, don't let rejection stop you. Only when you see failure as final, are you finally a failure. Take a look at your past experiences. You encountered rejection in school and on the playground. Not everyone liked you, but you made it anyway, right? Jesus experienced more rejection than anybody who ever lived. "He came unto his own, and his own received him not." Did He quit? No, He went on to others, to those who discerned His value.

Someone needs what you have; it is absolutely necessary to their success. **"But as many as received him, to them gave he power to become the sons of God," (John 1:11-12).** Jesus said, **"Whoever shall not receive you...shake off the dust of your feet," (Mt 10:14).** When you encounter rejection, in whichever form it may have come in your life, shake it off and move on. Sooner or later you will succeed if you don't quit. Don't personalize it. Because someone rejects what you have to *offer* doesn't mean they're rejecting *you*. Paul writes**: "For a great and effective door has opened to me, and there are many adversaries," (1 Cor. 16:9).** Opportunity and opposition-they go together. Life is not going to hand you success on a silver platter; you've got to overcome adversity and outlast the opposition in order to walk through the door. And only two things are required: Your faith and God's favor! *God controls it all.*

The Scripture says promotion doesn't come from people; promotion comes from God. When it's your time to be promoted or healed or restored, God doesn't check with your friends, your boss, or your family. As the angel told the ...Virgin Mary, God will make it happen without a man. If God can do it without a man, then He can do it without a bank. He can do it without medicine. You may have spent long enough considering your circumstances. It's time to start considering your God. He is the all-powerful Creator of the Universe. What He has spoken over your life may seem impossible. It may look too big. When you run the numbers, it may not seem logical. But don't overanalyze. Don't try to reason it out, because you'll talk yourself out of it.

In prison I had this unshakable faith, fully persuaded according to my identity in Christ that God is going to fulfill supernaturally, things in my life, as He has purposed to His glory. Not being able to afford a lawyer, I was going to have to face the judge and to request him to let me defend myself. Knowing full well that I had surrendered all things to God, I could do my part and depend on God's power within to lead. God has spoken and promised to show Himself strong. We must be like children relying on our heavenly Father's mighty arm. Like Paul, we could say that we have no confidence in the flesh but rejoice in Jesus Christ! (Philippians 3:2-3)

Author James P. Gills says: "We must think about how we think, especially in times of adversity. Victory becomes a question of our focus and our choice to orient ourselves appropriately to the elements of trust in God in every aspect of our life. We are blind and under the dark wrap of sin and selfishness when we are left to our own ways and "wisdom." Yet, we have the wonderful hope, as believers, that the Spirit of God can empower each of us to escape this darkness and to gain spiritual sight by simply seeking Him. We do this by reading the Word of God - His revealed wisdom - provides the answers we need, giving us true direction to guide our hearts into His glorious light.

God must quicken us, enabling us to change our motivation. When weak, disappointed, and facing sorrow, the believer can truly say, "Thy will be done" (looking to God in faith). In submission to God's sovereignty, you will experience strength and know fellowship with Christ in His sufferings. Then you will learn to exchange your weakness, as you wait on God for His strength and **"...mount up with wings like eagles..." (Isaiah 40:31).**

It is our part to see our weakness, in earnest desire and longing, convinced of the fact that we cannot help ourselves; we must trust God for divine enablement. *No one can rest until resting in Him.*

Satan's greatest deception might be that of blinding us to God's light and truth with negativity and attitudes of hopelessness and defeat. Perhaps the place of deepest darkness is a sense of isolation and abandonment in adversity. When filled with such feelings you may feel you cannot lift your eyes from your feet to move toward every pilgrim's wonderful destination - the Celestial City. Yet, it is only when we are brought to feel this extreme of hopelessness that we can see the greatest spiritual light God gives.

God offers freedom and shalom *(peace)* to those whose lives are completely surrendered to Him.

**According to the Scriptures, we must seek these graces: diligence, virtue, knowledge, self-control, perseverance, godliness, brotherly kindness, and love.** (See **2 Peter 1:9**) In His divine power, by grace, God gives us everything for life and godliness. **"The blessings of the LORD makes rich and He adds no sorrow with it," (Proverbs 10:22).** You will only experience tranquility and true joy when you have surrendered all to God. The Scriptures teach clearly what our motivation should be: **"Keep your heart with all diligence, for out of it spring the issues of life," (Proverbs 4:23).** Rejoicing in Christ can protect you from the temptation to complain. Count your blessings and name them one by one and it will surprise you what the Lord has done, look back and be thankful, see His promises for you and keep praising Him in advance by faith to see manifestation. Expect God to do great things in your life and through you for others. Live in faith, without faith it's impossible to please God. **"Know ye therefore that they which are of faith, the same are the children of Abraham. And the scripture, foreseeing that God would justify the heathen through faith, preached before the gospel unto Abraham, saying, In thee shall all nations be BLESSED. So then they which be of faith are BLESSED with faithful Abraham. V. 13-14. Christ hath redeemed us from the curse of the law, being made a curse for us: for it is written, Cursed is every one that hangeth on a tree: that THE BLESSING of Abraham might come on the Gentiles through Jesus Christ; that we might receive the promise of the Spirit through faith. V.26-29. For ye are all children of God by faith in Christ Jesus…And if ye be Christ's, then are ye Abraham's seed, and heir according to the promise." (Galatians 3:7-9)**

Author Kenneth Copeland in his book: THE BLESSING OF THE LORD writes, "We're the seed of that BLESSING! The promise is on us. Isaiah 51:3 is the Eden Covenant! It was the covenant between God and Adam before he sinned. God wants His Garden back. He intended for that Garden to be spread all over this planet until the Earth became the garden spot of the Universe."

Your place can be the garden spot of your universe. That was God's plan, and He never changes. He made man to live in a garden. And that should have been the worst environment man ever experienced because, "Eye hath not seen, nor ear heard, neither have entered into the heart of man, the things which God hath prepared for them that love him" (1 Corinthians 2:9). The Garden of Eden was just the starting point. It should have been expanded by Adam and Eve and their descendants into a greater and greater area, while God just observed His children at work because He had handed over the *power* and authority to continue to create that Garden all over the Earth.

**Christ's Finished Work on the Cross**

**"My Little children, these things I write unto you, that ye sin not. And if any man sin, we have an *advocate with the Father, Jesus Christ the righteous*. V9. He that saith he is in the light, and hateth his brother, is in darkness even until now. V.11 But he that hateth his brother is in darkness, and knoweth not wither he goeth, because that darkness hath blinded his eyes. V12 I write to you little children because your sins are forgiven you for his name's sake. V15 Love not the world, neither the things *that are* in the world. If any man love the world, the love of the Father is not in him. For all that *is* in the world, the lust of the flesh, and the lust of the eyes, and the pride of life, is not of the Father, but is of the world. And the world passeth away, and the lust thereof: but he that doeth the will of God abideth forever." (John 2:1 & v9, 12, 15-16)**

Because of Christ's finished work, Christians already possess the approval, the love, the security, the freedom, the meaning, the purpose, the protection, the new beginning, the cleansing, the forgiveness, the righteousness, and the rescue that we intensely long for and look for in a thousand things smaller than Jesus. These things may be every day things, yet are transient, meaning they are incapable of delivering the goods.

While I was in prison, although I was facing possible deportation, the more I let the waterfall of God's forgiveness and unmerited favor wash over me, the more I received soundness for my mind, the more l realized God was working it all out. Despite our efforts to contain, move past, or silence it, the Cross stands tall, resolutely announcing that, **"In all things God works for the good of those who love him, who have been called according to his purpose,"** (Romans 8: 28).

Whatever my outcome in my present situation, I now know my life in Christ is a life of forgiveness, rather than a life of condemnation, a life of eternal support rather than a life of fear, a life of promise rather than a life of panic. When Jesus said that He's the door, He promised more than just a way in. He said, **"Whoever enters through me will be saved. They will come in and go out, and find pasture,"** (John 10:9).

The Gospel is the only thing big enough to satisfy our deepest, eternal longing - both now and forever. Mankind's sin is deeper than we're ever willing to admit; it's mere spiritual blindness not to recognize and to celebrate our Savior Jesus Christ, whose righteousness is beyond our reach, but given to us for free. So often our focus on our circumstances instead of what Christ has done, blinds us and delays us from walking in our God-ordained destiny. Because we are so naturally prone to look at ourselves and our performance more than we do to Christ and His performance. We need constant reminders of the Gospel. The entrance of God's truth, His Word is so key in our spiritual sight. **"Praise be to the God and Father of our Lord Jesus Christ, who has blessed us in the heavenly realms with every spiritual blessing in Christ. For he chose us in him before the creation of the world to be holy and blameless in his sight. In love he predestined us for adoption to Sonship through Jesus Christ, in accordance with his pleasure and will – to the praise of his glorious grace, which he has freely given us in the One he loves. In him we have redemption through his blood, the forgiveness of sins, in accordance with the riches of God's grace that he lavished on us. With all wisdom and understanding, he made known to us the mystery of his will according to his good pleasure, which he purposed in Christ, to be put into effect** when the times reach their fulfillment – to bring unity to all things in heaven and on earth under Christ.

**In him we were also chosen, having been predestined according to the plan of him who works out everything in conformity with the purpose of his will, in order that we, who were the first to put our hope in Christ, might be for the praise of his glory. And you also were included in Christ when you heard the message of truth, the gospel of your salvation. When you believed, you were marked in him with a seal, the promised Holy Spirit, who is a deposit guaranteeing our inheritance until the redemption of those who are God's possession- to the praise of his glory." (Ephesians 1:3-14).** *Beauty for Ashes. God's amazing grace and mercy changes everything!*

I have no doubt in my mind that God used my season of unemployment to equip and strengthen me spiritually, preparing me for things that were about to unfold in my near future. If I did not have the sound backbone of His Word invested in me, I would have lost my mind or have been crushed; I would never have been able to come into the disturbing, heart-wrenching, hurtful wrong done to my family, and remain sane…but God's sure Word and His presence kept me standing, Praise the Lord! Like the Bible reminds us, faith comes by hearing and hearing (*constantly*), the Word of God.

Prior to my being imprisoned, I read the Bible and prayed a lot, including writing my first book, *Grace, Memoirs of Andeso.* Writing these books have been for me, a step of faith, mainly with the help of the Spirit of God. Glory to God! **"I will instruct you and teach you in the way you should go, I will counsel you with my loving eye on you" (Psalm 32:8)** And the spirit has continued to lead me step by step, therefore, it's the gospel (what Jesus has done) that alone can give God-honoring animation to our obedience. The power to obey comes from being moved and motivated by the completed work of Jesus for us. The fuel to do good flows from what's already been done. So, while the law directs, only the Gospel can drive us.

*Beauty for Ashes*

During this time of unemployment, I continued to be enlightened in the knowledge of God's Word, and some of the ways He operates in our lives when we're undergoing some kind of "wilderness." My husband was leaving me! My kids won't return my phone calls! My mother is in the hospital! I also got laid off! Beloved, do not be surprised at the fiery ordeal that is taking place. Nothing strange is happening to you. In fact, we are advised to, Rejoice! You are sharing Christ's sufferings!

**"Dear friends, do not be surprised at the fiery ordeal that has come on you to test you, as though something strange were happening to you. But rejoice inasmuch as you participate in the sufferings of Christ, so that you may be overjoyed when his glory is revealed. If you are insulted because of the name of Christ, you are blessed, for the Spirit of glory and of God rests on you. If you suffer, it should not be as a murderer or thief or any other kind of criminal, or even as a meddler. However, when you suffer as a Christian do not be ashamed, but praise God that you bear that name. For it is time for judgement to begin with God's household," (1 Peter 4:12-17).**

Now this seems to be the worst kind of response to someone in pain. "Suffering? Relax! It's no surprise...actually, you should be happy!" As insensitive as this sounds, don't let yourself think that Peter isn't following the example of God Himself. Consider the crucifixion. When Jesus told His disciples that He was going to be arrested, tried, convicted and executed, Peter said, "Never!" And Jesus' response was, "Get behind me, Satan." Remember, God works "under the opposite"- of where we think He will be. He worked in the crucifixion to save us. He worked in Peter's abandonment and denial to restore him, and He works in our struggles and in our hurt to give us joy.

Jesus told His followers that in this life they will have struggles. "But," He said "take heart! I have overcome the world" (John 16:33) He did not say that things would get better, although we wish He would (and sometimes things do). He simply said that He has overcome the world.

We suffer, but we never suffer alone. Jesus said that He came for the sick. The healthy have no need of him. We never suffer alone. And our suffering, stinging though it may be, not only has an end, its end has already been *assured*. **"The God of all grace, who called you to his eternal glory in Christ...will himself restore you and make you strong, firm and steadfast," (1 Pet. 5:10).** Remember today that you never suffer alone.

But it wasn't until I was imprisoned that the depth of God's everlasting love and purpose for my personal life, and the power of His message to us who are in "union with Christ" as Paul puts it in (Ephesians 1), gave me the courage and confidence I required to stand in faith. Not only for myself, but God gave me the boldness I needed while in prison to encourage the other inmates, and to bring them to salvation to reveal to and for them to rest on the truth that the "profound event" of the Gospel of Jesus Christ's life, death, and resurrection has happened; and that it alone can give us hope, and offer true perspective.

When we forgive others, who wrong us we become channels of God's grace and conductors of the same love that God has shown to us. God is at work in us when we forgive, without that divine work, we would become bitter and self-destructive. These spiritual blessings seem as foolishness to the unbeliever. The natural man is missing the best part of life, which is the reality and ecstasy of experiencing the gracious presence of God. Believers know what it means to dwell in the secret place of the Most High and to abide under the shadow of the Almighty **(Psalm 91:1).** We know what it means for God to draw near to us, to manifest Himself to us, and pour out His Spirit upon us as anointing oil from heaven. We may then say:

*The LORD make His face shine upon you, and be gracious to you;*

*The LORD lift up His countenance upon you, and give you peace.*

*Numbers 6:25-26*

If God has saved you - if He's given you the faith to believe, and you're now a Christian - then here's the good news:

you've already been qualified, you've already been delivered, you've already been transferred, you've already been redeemed, and you've already been forgiven.

As Paul writes, "in Christ with every spiritual blessing" (v.3 ESV): we've been chosen (v.4), graced (v.6), redeemed (v.7), reconciled (v.10), destined (v.11), and sealed forever (v. 13). Everything we need and long for, Paul says, we already possess if we are in Christ. He has already sweepingly secured all that our hearts crave. We no longer need to rely, therefore, on the position, the prosperity, the promotions, the preeminence, the power, the praise, the passing pleasures, or the popularity that we've so desperately pursued for so long. ***In Christ we have beauty for ashes.***

While in prison, after sharing the message of salvation constantly at different occasions fourteen people in total gave their lives to Christ, glory to God! On request, the prison granted us fourteen Bibles. Almost all of the new believers joined the Bible Study program offered by the prison. And I was able to really see yet again, that God makes "all things" to work together for good. Though not all things are God sent, all things are God used. "**See to it, brothers and sisters, that none of you has a sinful, unbelieving heart that turns away from the living God. But encourage one another daily, as long as it is called 'Today,' so that none of you maybe hardened by sin's deceitfulness. We have come to share in Christ, if indeed we hold our original conviction firmly to the very end," (Hebrews 3:12-14).**

In prison we started holding prayer sessions and praying for each other. Apart from that, the prison had preachers who came in twice every week. So, let us pray, have quiet times, fast, worship, and do a myriad of things to cultivate our relationship with our Savior. But let us never worry that He is absent or estranged, for He has assured us that He will be with us "always, even to the end of the age" (See **Matt. 28:20 NASB**) For Christians, then, it is not "practice makes perfect." It's something closer to "Christ's perfection frees you to practice." In Him, our relationship is always secure, and in Him, our practice, whatever it is, is made perfect.

Psalm 26 was written by David - the same David who murdered Uriah in order to take Bathsheba as his wife. So, what happened? How can this man write these things about himself?

The answer can be found in a single sentence spoken to David when his crime became public. The prophet Nathan reveals David's sin to him, causing him to say, simply, "I have sinned against the LORD." It's the sentence that Nathan then speaks over David that allows him to proclaim his innocence in Psalm 26 despite being anything but: "The LORD has taken away your sin. You are not going to die." (2 Sam. 12:13)

For us it is at the Cross of Christ, in the blood of the Savior spilled for us, that we are washed clean and declared innocent. David was told that God would not hold his sins against him. We are told, through Christ and the Cross that we are made innocent, through the innocence of Him who died for us. And so, we remember the One who came to die, the One who came to trade His righteousness, his innocence, for our sin, for our guilt. Looking to the Cross, we can say with David and Psalm 26, "Do not take away my soul along with sinners." (v.9), and know that, in Christ, it is finished, and we, therefore, are innocent before God.

# CHAPTER EIGHT

## Pray Without Ceasing

"It is a good thing that we are commanded to pray, or else in times of heaviness we might give it up. If God commands me, unfit as I may be, I creep to the footstool of grace, and since He says, 'Pray without ceasing,' though my heart fails me and my heart itself will wander, yet I will still stammer out the wishes of my hungering soul and say, **'O God, at least teach me to pray and help me to prevail with You.'** " By: Charles Spurgeon's words.

### Switch Your Thoughts with God's Word

The devil will continually torment you in your mind. You possess the ultimate weapon to fight back, in this battle of the mind – the Word of God, which is the Sword of the Spirit. So, put on the full armor of God. **"For though we live in the world, we do not wage war as the world does. The weapons we fight with are not weapons of the world. On the contrary, they have divine power to demolish strongholds. We demolish arguments and every pretension that sets itself up against the knowledge of God, and we take captive every thought to make it obedient to Christ. And we will be ready to punish every act of disobedience, once your obedience is complete,"** (1 Cor.10:4-6).

This war rages on, it is how we are wired. Fill yourself with God's Word and fight back every defeating, destroying or daunting thought that aims to destruct you from your true identity in Christ according to His promises for you, in the written Word.

Defeating thoughts, like how was I going to be able to support my aging mother? How was I going to pay the medical insurance that she so desperately needed? How about money for paying for her medication? It's hard to get a job in Kenya, what if I do not get employment? You're such a loser? You've failed at everything? The battle in my mind was raging on, and on and on. Satan wants you to remove God out of the equation, he wants you to think that you make life happen in your own strength and effort. But the truth be told, it has always been the Lord who takes care of His children.

It is God who gives us the knowledge, health and strength to get wealth; it's prideful not to acknowledge Him in all areas of our lives. Praising Him in both the good times and the bad because He makes all things to work together for good to those who love Him in Christ Jesus. God commands victories for His people, and all things are His servants. Our God is a Father who acts on behalf of the one who puts his hope in Him. He is at work to answer our prayers in His good way and time.

God used me to be a blessing to my mother just as much as He used my other sisters and my brother David, and God also made countless other means available blessings in her life to His glory, but the point is…all along: **"For it is God who works in you to will and to act in order to fulfill his good purpose," (Philippians 2:13).** And that is why God warns us not to take the glory that is due Him. **"But may it never be that I should boast, except in the cross of our Lord Jesus Christ…" (Galatians 6:14)** Every good gift comes from God, without Him, we have nothing. The fact that we are even alive, in good health, we have a source of income, a roof over our head and can afford to put food on the table…is something that we need to be thankful for daily, that we can wake up and see another day, is a miracle in itself! Be thankful and extend your appreciation to your Creator, God Almighty!

You are not the job you have, the car you drive or the house you live in. The truth is that you are a spiritual being created in the image of God, having a human experience. *And what God says is…Remember Me, remember my love for you, remember what I have done for you!* "I love you" is a phrase of well-known power. But there's a problem: we don't believe that we can be loved, especially by God. God's "I love you" can feel even more evasive than "the mankind-love." His standards certainly seem higher. While in "the man kind-love" we never have to turn the other cheek, do we? We don't have to love with all our heart, soul, mind, and strength, do we? These are the things we think are required of us for God's "I love you" to apply. So, when someone says, "God loves you" we smirk inside. It feels trite and forced. It feels manipulative. We act as if God's "I love you" will be revoked if we don't deserve it.

The good news is that God's "I love you" is proclaimed specifically to those who don't deserve it. In other words, we don't need a makeover to be loved by God. God's "I love you" is based on the deserving of another, our Lord and Savior Jesus Christ. God demonstrates his love in this: **"While we were still sinners, Christ died for us" (Rom.5:8).** On the Cross, Christ's righteousness was given to us and our sin was laid upon Him. God's "I love you," aimed at His perfect Son, is ours forever. *God give us Beauty for Ashes.*

The fact that we choose to continue to be ignorant of who we are, why we are here, and where our help comes from is spiritual blindness, and does not stop life from happening to us. Sooner or later we quickly realize that only God is in control and in charge. Armed with the knowledge that we, like everyone else, are in open rebellion, we come - once again-face-to-face with our need for a Savior. Whether we flout the rules or love them, we need salvation. In Christ, we have just such a Savior. He silences our internal lawyers by satisfying His eternal law.

See, the many times I didn't have anything to support my aging mother, God who had always been her true supplier continued to supply, and never once let her down because of my unemployment. Mom has lived with the verse, "The just shall live by faith" close to her heart and God has not once failed her. But as long as I saw myself as the one who provided for her, when I had no income, the devil used fear, worry and anxiety to torment me. Friends and relatives talked about me having abandoned my mother…that hurt, but you know God knows all things, you don't have to defend yourself before people, guard your heart. "Blessed is the man who trusts in the LORD, whose confidence is in him. He will be like a tree planted by the water that sends out its roots by the stream. It does not fear when heat comes; its leaves are always green. It has no worries in a year of drought and never fails to bear fruit. **(Jeremiah 17:7-8)**

Heat will come, and drought will come. The word of God says rejoice in your sufferings, because you know that suffering produces perseverance; perseverance, character, and character, hope**, (Romans 5:3-5)**. We have the Comforter, when we cooperate with Him, the Spirit of God will guide us through times of suffering. And besides the Scriptures teach: **"Can any one of you by worrying add a single hour to your life? V.33 But seek first his kingdom and his righteousness, and all these things will be given to you as well. Therefore do not worry about tomorrow for tomorrow will worry about itself. Each day has enough trouble of its own,"** (Mathew 6:27 & 33-34).

The Lord desires that we seek Him in all matters pertaining to all areas of our lives, and then trust Him to take care of us. God wants to be our trusted and unlimited source of supply. But the spirit of pride blinds us, and we think that we are what it takes for another human being to be able to stand. The devil is a liar and uses that lie to get us to panic when we are in lack and no longer in control. And then, he uses the same reasons to cause us to be depressed, to worry and to give ourselves the credit that is due God. In the process we fail to thank Him, praise Him for His continued faithfulness under very trying circumstances, but Our God remains faithful, yesterday, today and forever and He does not change, nor does He treat us, as our sins deserve.

# CHAPTER NINE

## Knowing the Lord

The more we study the Word of God, the more we know His voice, the easier it becomes to distinguish His voice apart from the enemy's luring, defeating voice that is always tending to draw you to a place of discouragement, worry and anxiety. None of us knows everything we need to know about the ways of God. That's why it's important for us to continue to study the Word and to be transformed. **"Be not conformed to this world: but be transformed by the renewing of your mind," (Romans 12:2).** We must have enough Word in us to fight back. We've all been brought up in the worldly fleshly ways of thinking, and the world's ways are in opposition to the ways of God. There's no agreement between the Spirit and the flesh. **"For they that are after the flesh do mind the things of the flesh; but they that are after the Spirit the things of the Spirit. For to be carnally minded is death; but to be spiritually minded is life and peace. Because the carnal mind is enmity against God: for it is not subject to the law of God, neither indeed can be," (Romans 8:5-7).** These verses tell us we can either think carnally, or we can think spiritually. Since being spiritually minded is the key to life and peace, the more spiritually minded we become, the more successful, prosperous and victorious we'll be able to live the abundant life Christ died for us to live.

The reverse is also true. The more carnally minded we are, the less victorious we'll be. The more defeated we'll be. So, if some things aren't working in our lives, we need to check our thinking. When we do things the world's way, we get the world's results, and that's no fun because the world is in a mess. It's being ruled by the devil. It is operating under condemnation and the law of sin and death. As believers, we are not supposed to be living under the law of sin and death! We've been redeemed from that law as Romans 8:1-2 says.

Why aren't believers living in that kind of freedom? Because to experience that freedom, we must do more than just become born-again. We have to walk after the Spirit. If we keep on walking after the flesh, if we neglect to renew our minds with God's Word and learn to walk in agreement with His will, we will not have freedom. That means the devil will deceive us into trusting in our own strength, believing that we have it altogether, imposing his will on us. He'll keep us thinking and focused on what we can see in the natural realm, but God desires that we gain spiritual sight. It's easy to focus on what we don't have. Often people say they don't have any talent, no education, or the personality they'd like to have, but as long as you think you're lacking, it will keep you from God's best.

Author Joel Osteen writes: "It's not enough to just have faith in God. That's important, but you should take it a step further and have faith in what God has given you. Don't make excuses; you have to believe you are equipped. You are empowered. You have the talent, the amount of education, or the amount of money. What makes the difference is God's anointing on your life. You can have average talent but when God breathes in your direction, you'll go further than someone with exceptional talent. God is still on the throne and honors His Word. God requires our total trust. He promises that His Word will not return to Him void? Why not give God a chance, you've tried everything else, you owe it to yourself." **"For my thoughts *are* not your thoughts, neither are your ways my ways," saith the LORD. "For as the heavens are higher than the earth, so are my ways higher than your ways, and my thoughts than your thoughts. For *as* the rain cometh down, and the snow from heaven, and returneth not thither, but watereth the earth, and maketh it bring forth and bud, that it may give seed to the sower, and bread to the eater. So shall my word be that goeth forth out of my mouth: it shall not return to me void, but it shall accomplish that which I please, and it shall prosper *in the thing* whereto I sent it."(Isaiah 55:8-11)**

God's Word is truth and will stand firm forever. His Word will accomplish all things according to His plan in your life and mine. His will, will be done! **"Since you died with Christ to the elemental spiritual forces of this world, why, as though you still belonged to the world, do you submit to its rules: "Do not handle! Do not taste! Do not touch!"? These rules, are based on merely human commands and teachings. Such regulations indeed have an appearance of wisdom, with their self-imposed worship, their false humility and their harsh treatment of the body, but they lack any value in restraining sensual indulgence,"(Colossians 2:20-23).**

If we trust God fully, we will find the perfect peace and joy that will prevent our self-destruction. Our whole task in life is to trust Him with the whole mind, heart, and spirit. As the prophet, Habakkuk, says, we must learn to trust God regardless of what happens.

**"Though the fig tree may not blossom, Nor fruit be on the Vines; Though the labor of the olive may fail, And the fields Yield no food; Though the flock may be cut off from the Fold, And there be herd in the stalls- Yet will I rejoice In the LORD, I will rejoice in the God of my salvation. The LORD God is my strength; He will make my feet like deer's Feet, And He will make me walk on my high hills." (HABAKKUK 3:17-19)**

# CHAPTER TEN

## The Battle of Your Mind

There are no good enough reasons why we make poor, destructive choices, except that we are sinful people, loved by a gracious God! In my situation the consequences could end up costing me everything. My hope in God became everything that changed everything. Let us learn from our mistakes, and always remember that God has a plan for our lives. He has all the intentions to fulfill it to the end. And so I thank God that even though I have many flaws, I belong to God who is wonderful through and through, and the Holy Spirit, my wonderful Counsellor, my ever-present help in trouble, immediately available around the clock, the only One whose love is flawless...the only One who is worthy of my highest praise. O God, who is like You? There is none to compare with You! **"Because he loves me," says the LORD, "I will rescue him; I will protect him, for he acknowledges my name, He will call on me, and I will answer him; I will be with him in trouble, I will deliver him and honor him. With long life I will satisfy him and show him my salvation," (Psalm 91:14-16)**. You do what you know to do right, and that is to stand on the Word. Even if your present circumstances look bad, they may be your reality at this moment, but what determines you winning this battle or losing the battle is the way you choose to respond to your circumstances. That is what determines if you will continue to live your life making the same mistakes, or you will use your circumstances as a stepping-stone to the next level in your life.

There is a real battle taking place in your mind. This is the place where the enemy launches attacks against you and me, in your thoughts and imagination. Of course, there will be consequences by law for any irresponsible behavior. That should not stop you from standing on the Word and taking refuge in God. The law will punish your sin, life will make you pay for your bad choices, and you can count on it! God's love on the other hand is everlasting and never changes. He will strengthen you, and He'll walk with you through your storm as you put your trust in Him. He will cause all things to work together for your good, even your pain. **"Whoever dwells in the shelter of the Most High will rest in the shadow of the Almighty. I will say of the LORD, "He is my refuge and my fortress, my God, in whom I trust," (Psalm 91:1-2).**

Emotions are real and they are to be acknowledged under the circumstances. But God did not create us to be overcome by our circumstances but to overcome our circumstances by faith in Him and in the power of His Word by believing He is going to do what He promises His children. In other words, we are to seek first the Kingdom of God. You do not go by the way you feel, feelings are meant to draw you in, and to lure you to think low of yourself, give-up, believe what others have said about you, be fearful when things are out of your control and wounds of old erupt. This can include prolonged sorrow when loved ones depart. Sometimes life's journey will overwhelm us...looking back, you can see some times of ease and refreshment.

Looking ahead, however, you see only a continuing ascent. The top of the mountain you are climbing is nowhere in sight. All of this just distracts our focus from where our focus should be, on the Lord ... Who delivers us. He is the only One who knows how hard it is for you to keep going day after day. And so, He says, **"Do not become weary and discouraged in your soul."** See, **"Consider Him who endured such hostility from sinners against himself, lest you become weary and discouraged in your souls," (Hebrews 12:3 NKJV).** Most likely fear, worry, anxiety and depression sets in...God's Word tells us in no uncertain terms that the warfare takes place in our minds and is won by God's Word, "... **pulling down strongholds, casting down arguments and every high thing that exalts itself against the knowledge of God, bringing every thought into captivity to the obedience of Christ," (2 Cor. 10:4-5).**

The Author Joseph Prince says, "Once you are aware that there is a war for your mind, and that it is between wrong beliefs and right beliefs, you have already won half the battle! Yes things look bad, you're in trouble with the law, you have no rent or mortgage, your marriage is in trouble, the doctor's report is devastating, a child has gone wayward; in short, life just isn't working out for you…you live in a culture dedicated to entertainment and pleasure-seeking. In such a climate, a life of struggle feels alien. If you are not careful, you will succumb to self-pity, a sinful snare, remember the devil only has one mission and one mission alone, to destroy *you.* He has come to kill, to steal and to destroy you, ***but Christ came that you may have life and have life more abundantly.*** To avoid falling into this trap, remember that God is Sovereign, and He is lovingly present with you. **"The LORD appeared to us in the past, saying: 'I have loved you with an everlasting love; I have drawn you with loving-kindness.' " (Jeremiah 31:3)** Your ongoing struggle is not a mistake or a punishment. Try to view it, instead, as a rich opportunity: Your uphill journey keeps you aware of your neediness, so you look to the Lord for help!"

# CHAPTER ELEVEN

## Awaiting Rescue

Going back to when I was awaiting my trial, not knowing what the outcome would be for me, I trustingly whispered the name JESUS, over and over again, it *is* the Name above all names! At the name of Jesus Christ every knee shall bow, and every tongue confess that Jesus Christ is LORD! I kept His praise continually in my mouth; I felt embraced in everlasting love. **"There is no fear in love; but perfect love casteth out fear, because fear hath torment. He that feareth is not made perfect in love. We love him, because he first loved us," (1 John 4:18-19 NIV).** Although there are aspects of our identity in Christ that the enemy seems to challenge the most, I believe the God Who chose you and I in Christ Jesus will not let our momentary troubles stand in the way of our God given destiny.

When the Lord is training His children in the discipline of perseverance, it may seem like we are on a long uphill journey, which sometimes seems endless. **"Sing the praises of the LORD, you his faithful people; praise his holy name. For his anger lasts a moment, but his favor lasts a lifetime; weeping may stay for the night but rejoicing comes in the morning." (Psalm 30:4-5)**

When I appeared before the judge, it's amazing how peaceful I felt. For one, I knew I was not alone in that courtroom, God promises never to leave us nor forsake us, believe He's with you. **"Even though I walk through the darkest valley, I will fear no evil for you are with me; your rod and your staff, they comfort me," (Psalm 23:4).** The previous days I had spent time seeking direction, in prayer and fasting. The morning of my day in court, the Lord impressed upon my heart to: **"Be still and know that I am God."** (Ps.46:10) *It's all we need to hear, what comfort!* I used to think that when Paul told us to "work out [our] salvation" (Phil. 2:12), it meant go out and get what you don't have-get more patience, get more strength, get more joy, get more love, and so on. But after reading the Bible more carefully, I now understand that Christian growth does not happen by working hard to get something you don't have. *Rather, Christian growth happens by working hard to daily swim in the reality of what you do have. Believing again and again and again that the Gospel of God's free justifying grace every day is the hard work we're called to.*

To the judge and the prosecutor, I answered each and every question honestly. I took responsibility and owned up to my part to the wrongdoing. Their questions forced me to address my painful past that I'd avoided to talk about, except to the Lord in prayer. After the interrogation and the testimony, the judge set me free. Amazingly, he wished me luck and encouraged me in the steps I had already taken in my life.

When we go to the Lord with humility and a repentant heart, He forgives us and leads us the right way. **"If My people, which are called by My name, shall humble themselves, and pray, and seek My face, and turn from their wicked ways; then will I hear from heaven, and will forgive their sin, and will heal their land," (2 Chr. 7:14).** Prayer is the only pathway to *the peace of God.* **"Be careful for nothing; but in everything by prayer and supplication with thanksgiving let your requests be made known unto God. And the peace of God, which passeth all understanding, shall keep your hearts and minds through Christ Jesus," (Phil.4:6, 7).**

A superficial faith, not based on Scripture, fails to acknowledge God in moments of need. We must learn to see spiritually by choosing to walk in the Lord's design rather than our own. *This* walk of trust is what it means to be a Christian. In true faith we trust God, while in the conventional sight of the mind, we lack such trust and are blind. God's words act differently than human words: Our words can encourage or discourage, build up or put down, buoy or sink. God's words create and destroy. God's first word (the Law) destroys us. It cuts us to the quick and ends our lives. God's second word, the Gospel, is just as powerful - it makes all things new (Rev.21:5).

# CHAPTER TWELVE

## Just Come

When we thirst for a relationship with God, we participate in the things that are meant to get God interested in us. We think that the good we do will cause God to take notice of us. We pray; we read the Bible; we serve those less fortunate. We work...Religious people are wired this way. Jesus basically tells us, "If you thirst, just come. Come as you are. Come thirsty, come in need. *After* you get close to Me, *then* out of your heart will flow the good works." He's reversing the order! We think it's our good works that bring us close to God, when in fact it's our closeness to God that produces good works. If you're thirsty, drink. If you're hungry, eat. If you are a sinner, *be saved.* It is Christ's, and through Christ, it is yours. **(Ephesians 2:8-10)**

First things first – seeking first the kingdom of God and His righteousness. Maybe you are reading this book and have not yet invited Jesus Christ in your heart as your Savior...I would like to let you know, salvation is the most important decision you will ever make for yourself. Don't worry about all that you do or don't do that's imperfect, *no human being is going to ever be perfect,* **only Jesus is perfect**.

We start every New Year thinking...*This is the year!* We resolve to turn over a new leaf-and this time we're serious. We promise ourselves that we are going to quit bad habits and start good ones. We're going to get in shape, eat better, waste less time, and be more content, disciplined, and international. We're going to be better husbands, wives, fathers, and mothers. We're going to pray more, serve more, plan more, give more, read more, and memorize more Bible verses. We're going to finally be all that we can be. No more messing around. *And then, twelve months later, we realize we've fallen short-again.*

We have to realize that it's not by our determination, otherwise the change is very temporary. Thank God that our influence and our victories are not by human might or power, but by the Spirit of God. But oh, what happens when we praise God and bring our requests to Him in simple faith, when we plug into His almighty power…when we offer a sacrifice of thanksgiving to honor the Lord? We open a door for Him to rescue us and bless our lives, and we prepare the way for Him to rescue and bless other people, near and far. In the Scriptures we read such confidence is only found in Christ Jesus; **"Such confidence we have through Christ before God. Not that we are competent in ourselves to claim anything for ourselves, but our competence comes from God. He has made us competent as ministers of a new covenant-not of the letter but of the Spirit; for the letter kills, but the Spirit gives life," (2 Cor.3:4-6).**

On our own we cannot change ourselves, break old habits, or our sinful nature; this is done only through salvation *IN* Christ. God then through the power of the Holy Spirit begins His continuous work of transformation on the believer, from glory to glory to glory. Don't let your shortcomings be the excuse, or reason you do not commit your life to Christ today. I cannot stress enough how important this is; your very soul depends on it! How long will you falter between two opinions? Are you reading these words, realizing you are on the fence and you can't bring yourself to make a decision? Choose God! He will not fail you or forsake you - He loves you and has a plan for your life. Decide to follow Him. And remember, not to decide…really is to decide! There is no salvation in any other name, but in the name of Jesus Christ.

And there's no other way to God but through His Son Jesus Christ. **"Thomas said to him, 'Lord, we don't know where you are going, so how can we know the way?' Jesus answered, 'I am the way, the truth, and the life. No one comes to the Father except through me,' " (John 14:6-7).** Jesus came to Earth to be grace in the face of the world's judgment, to be love in the face of the world's critique, to be the Gospel in the face of the Law and to be God's "yes" to us. Jesus came to Earth to **"bring good news to the oppressed, to bind up the brokenhearted, to proclaim**

**liberty to the captives, and release to the prisoners; to proclaim the year of the LORD's favor," (Isaiah 61:1-2).**

It doesn't really take much for the devil to bring you down to his level. The temptation for Christians is to think that once God saves us, we move beyond the first "Adamic" impulse to fall upward. The truth is, however, that even after God saves us, we continue to fall upward, trying to claim for ourselves the glory that belongs to God alone. *John Stott wrote, "Man asserts himself against God and puts himself where only God deserves to be. God sacrifices himself for man and puts Himself where man deserves to be. The first Adam ventured up into the 'realm of things above' and brought death. The second Adam ventured down into the 'realm of things below' and brought life."* His gift of life is yours and mine today.

There are times or days, as human-beings, when we are vulnerable. When I was in prison there were challenging days and moments, times when l allowed defeating thoughts to cross my mind. Times when l wondered how my life would turn out? Thank God that as a child of God am never meant to bear my burdens, and yet after the fall, self-reliance became our default mode of operation. Fortunately, God does not leave us there. The Gospel is for the defeated, not the dominant. In view of God's holiness, we are all losers. **"For all have sinned and fall short of the glory of God," (Rom.3:23).** The good news of suffering is that it brings us to the end of ourselves. It brings us to the place of honesty, which is the place of desperation, the place of faith, the place of sovereign freedom. Suffering leaves our idols in pieces on the ground. It puts us in a position to see God sent His Son not only to suffer in our place but also to suffer with us. Our merciful friend has been through it all. He is with us right now! And while, He may not deliver us from pain and loss, He'll walk with us through it.

That God should allow His creature to have fellowship with Him is wonderful enough; but that He can desire it, that it gives Him satisfaction and joy and pleasure, is almost too much for my understanding. God desires His children to come boldly to His throne of grace, assured of His glad welcome- not because we're worthy or because we've served Him, but because He's a God of grace, a God of unmerited, unlimited favor-not little dribbles of favor reluctantly measured out, but overflowing, super-abundant favor. God welcomes us just as we are, simply because Jesus is our risen Savior, and we are alive with His life and righteous with His righteousness!

I began to thank the Lord that Christ is my life, and that I am a member of His body and a dwelling place of His spirit. How privileged I am to be indwelt by the whole Trinity: (God the Father, the Son and Holy Spirit)! And so, I thank God and offer my requests in detail, with thanksgiving…that I can pour out my heart before Him, being honest with Him about my feelings and my mistakes and my sins, seeing all He has seen me through, l turn to Him as my Lord and confess my sins rather than hiding them or clinging to them. His forgiveness is immediate and total…I never need to fear that God will judge or condemn me. When we transfer our fears, anxiety, worry or anger, and instead, take our burdens from our shoulders to His, we are able to find rest in Him as He works in us, for us and through us!

Though the work of Christ is finished for the sinner, it is not yet finished in the sinner. He is still working in me. in my every weakness. That is why I was able to thank God for this ***"enemy",*** in God's gracious plan to bless and use me, he's allowed me to go through hard times, through trials that many people go through in this fallen world. How so glad l am that the LORD is so good at reaching down and making something beautiful out of even the worst situations! But most importantly, comes the assurance that I am not forsaken and alone; He's with me in my valley. **"The LORD is my shepherd, I lack nothing. He makes me lie down in green pastures, he leads me beside quiet waters, and He refreshes my soul. He guides me along the right paths for his name's sake. Even though I walk through the darkest valley, I will fear no evil, for you are with me; your rod and your staff, they comfort me. You prepare a table before me in the presence of my enemies."(Psalm 23:1-5)**

Venting anger does not only affect those you love, and those around you, it affects you as well. In the Scriptures, Jesus gives a solution to those of us who are weary and heavily burdened: **"Come to me, all you who are weary and burdened, and I will give you rest. Take my yoke upon you and learn from me, for I am gentle and humble in heart, and you will find rest for your souls. For my yoke is easy and my burden is light,"(Mathew 11:28-30).** Self-pity is self-centeredness that diverts the focus that is meant to be on Christ, and instead focuses on self. The key to getting out of a cycle of sin and defeat is to receive God's unconditional love, and to stop beating yourself up. Receive God's love and stop punishing yourself because your sins have already been punished on the body of another-His name is Jesus, our beautiful Lord and Savior. No wonder the Gospel is called the *Good News*.

### The Prodigal Son and His Brother

The real star in the parable of the prodigal son is the father. He had two boys. One was rebellious; the other was religious. But he loved each of them. And because they were his family, he refused to give up on them. While the younger brother was away wallowing in sin, the older brother was at home wallowing in self-righteousness. One was guilty of the sins of the flesh (the obvious ones); the other was guilty of the sins of the spirit (the-not-so-obvious ones.) Only when the younger brother lost everything, did he discover that living in submission to his father's rule was the safest, most fulfilling place you can be. Only when the older brother discovered the difference between rule-keeping and relationship, was he able to understand his father's word, **"Everything I have is yours," (Luke 15:31 NIV)**. One was a miserable rule keeper; the other was a miserable rule breaker. (Which are you?) The problem was, neither one really knew the heart of their father because they were self-centered.

But that changed when they discovered that he loved them in spite of their flaws and planned to bless them. Understand this: you can read the Bible, go to church, keep all the rules-and not really know God's faithfulness, His love, and His plan for you. Until you really know God, you'll have no anchor in life; you'll be

*Beauty for Ashes*

tossed to and fro by circumstances, emotion and temptation. But when you know whose you are, you'll begin to understand who you are, what you're supposed to do, and where you're supposed to be.

Many of us, even as we progress toward full faith, may discover that we have been embittered through life situations in our dealings with other people. As human beings we tend to be embarrassed, hide or downplay our hurt, or things that happened in the past beyond our control. There may be offenses that might have occurred during childhood, as teenagers, or at middle age. Some things that might still be bondages, addictions, prolonged sicknesses, failures, grievous sins, or even generational curses that continue to be passed down from generation to generation. We can easily identify these curse patterns when we observe our family tree. **"But it shall come to pass, if thou wilt not harken unto the voice of the Lord thy God, to observe to do all his commandments and his statutes which I command thee this day; that all these curses shall come upon thee, and overtake thee."(Deuteronomy 28:15)**

As illustrated in the creation of the Earth in Genesis 1, everything reproduces after its own kind. We acknowledge this principle in buying pedigreed animals, but we completely ignore this principle when we deal with people. At the doctor's we are asked our family history which helps them figure out our *disposition-to lean a certain way*. Since the transgression of Adam, all families came under a curse. However, God made provision for you and future generations! **"Yet it pleased the Lord to bruise him; he hath put him to grief: when thou shalt make his soul an offering for sin, he shall see his seed, he shall prolong his days, and the pleasure of the Lord shall prosper in his hand. He shall see of the travail of his soul, and shall be satisfied: by his knowledge shall my righteous servant justify many; for he shall bear their iniquities.**

**Therefore will I divide him a portion with the great, and he shall divide the spoil with the strong; because he hath poured out his soul unto death: and he was numbered with the transgressors; and he bare the sin of many, and made intercession for the transgressors." (Isaiah 53:10-12)** Christ is the Answer to mankind's Salvation! The precious spotless blood of Jesus Christ cleanses us from all unrighteousness. Submit your will to God, knowing that Jesus suffered the curse and overcame the devil for you. Finally understand that God has all authority and delegated it to Jesus who has given it to you as a believer. Use your authority of the name of Jesus, declaring the power of the blood of Jesus. Declare that your family's generational curses are broken and speak blessings over your life and the lives of your children!

All these burdens weigh us down through the course of life. God through the power of the Holy Spirit is able to bring healing from past wounds and hurts which have controlled your behavior and speech that has caused damage in relationships. Let go of those past painful experiences and anything that would prevent you from walking out the perfect will of God. By taking everything to God in prayer, and having total trust in who God is, and what He is able to do in you, for you, and through you, you will see the salvation of the Lord at work in your life and some of the things eradicated in completeness, overturned and arrested by the blood of Jesus!

Author Paula White writes: "Curses produce bad and harmful results. Blessings produce good, beneficial results. Blessings and curses are not limited to the individual, but extend to families, tribes, communities and whole nations. Once released, they continue from generation to generation, until something happens to cancel their effect. (Galatians 3:13-14) says; **"...Christ redeemed us from the curse of the law, having become a curse for us (for it is written, cursed is everyone who hangs on a tree), that the blessing of Abraham might come upon the Gentiles in Christ Jesus, that we might receive the promise of the Spirit through faith."** The exchange from generational curse to generational blessing is passed to us by the blood of Jesus Christ. Although life and blessing have been provided- the choice is yours for what you will live in. Have you wondered why you love God, but "life" is not working? We don't exercise the authority given us as believers in Christ. Another facet of salvation and our walk with Christ that is vital to our victory...the exchange from curse to blessing. God in His word says; **"My people are** destroyed for lack of knowledge..." (Hosea 4:6) We have to make a choice; God has given mankind a free will to choose. Not choosing God is automatically placing yourself under the curse. **"And if it seem evil unto you to serve the LORD, choose you this day whom you will serve, whether the gods which your fathers served that were on the other side of the flood, or the gods of the Amorites in whose land ye dwell:"( Joshua 24:15)**

At the Cross, an exchange took place that was divinely ordained by God! Jesus was punished that we might be forgiven. Jesus was wounded that we might be healed, and He was made sin that we might be made righteous with His righteousness. He died our death that we might share His life. Jesus was made a curse that we may receive the blessing, He endured shame that we might share His glory. He endured poverty that we may share His abundance. Jesus endured our rejection that we might enjoy acceptance. Our old man died in Jesus that our new man might live in Christ. There is more to salvation than simply "going to heaven". Salvation means to be physically healed, to be delivered or rescued, to recover from fatalities, ongoing preservation, protection and eternal life. *God gives us Beauty for Ashes!*

### Becoming Born Again

**"Most assuredly, I say to you, unless one is born again, he cannot see the kingdom of God," (John 3:3)**. How can a man be born again when he is old? And this question was asked by a man named Nicodemus, who was the epitome of moral righteousness and theological acumen, yet he had entirely missed the point of Jesus teaching. Jesus was not speaking of a physical birth, but of a spiritual birth. He went on to say: "That which is born of the flesh is flesh, and that which is born of the Spirit is spirit... **"You must be born again," (v. 6-7)**. Nicodemus had it all, yet he knew there must be something more to life than all of his head knowledge. After hearing the miraculous reports about Jesus, Nicodemus approached Him that night, humbled himself, and said to the lowly Galilean: "Rabbi, we know that You are a teacher come from God; for no one can do these signs that You do unless God is with Him" **(v. 2)**. Nicodemus definitely had an abundance of head knowledge. What Nicodemus needed was what each of us needs: a new heart. And so, he approached Jesus, hoping that in the darkness of night, he might find the light of truth. Nicodemus had spent his entire life studying, teaching, and applying the Word of God. Now, before his very eyes, was the *Word Incarnate*.

Jesus said to Nicodemus - and His message applies to you and me -"Do not marvel that I say to you, **"You must be born again," (v. 7)**. It is not an option. It is a command, an imperative. We who desire to see and to enter the kingdom of God must be born again. The Apostle Paul, a member of the Sanhedrin himself, later described this as being **"transformed" (Romans 12:2)**. We get our English word metamorphosis from this single compound Greek word. The picture is of a caterpillar spinning a cocoon around itself and later emerging as a new creation, a beautiful butterfly. No longer doomed and destined to crawl on its belly, this butterfly can now soar above the trees. Similarly, we experience a new birth when we recognize our sin, repent of that sin, and trust in Christ alone to forgive us. Yes, we MUST be born again.

What about Nicodemus? Did he become a follower of Christ that night? There is ample evidence in John 19 that, indeed, he did. As Jesus' body hung in death upon the Cross, two men arrived, removed the spikes from His wrists and feet, took the mocking crown of thorns from His head, lowered Him from the Cross, carried His body to the tomb, prepared Him for burial, and placed His lifeless body into the tomb. One of these men was the wealthy Joseph of Arimathea in whose tomb the body was placed. And the other man? "[It was] Nicodemus, who at first came to Jesus by night…Then [Nicodemus and Joseph] took the body of Jesus, and bound it in strips of linen with spices, as the custom of the Jews is to bury" **(vv.39-40)**. Yes, **"if anyone is in Christ, he is a new creation; old things have passed away; behold, all things have become new." (2 Corinthians 5:17)**

A man can't be born a second time physically, but Christ can take out your old heart and put in a brand-new one. This new birth is a spiritual birth. You MUST be born again. It is not an option but a necessity for anyone who will inherit eternal life. No one-not even a righteous Pharisee, much less a rough prostitute-is exempt from this divine call and command. The new birth is God's gift to you. Receive it. By faith, come to Jesus! Throughout this book, every so many chapters I write about the message of salvation, the Gospel. It's the good news. God's gracious gift to you and me!

## Forgive and Move On

Over the course of time we get hurt and we hurt others; we're betrayed by friends and loved ones, mislead, abused, sometimes we suffer due to other people's poor choices, self-inflicted wounds and heartache. Not to mention consequences of those past mistakes we made, or decisions our forefathers made that haunt us through those generational curses. Even when we are not to blame, we have to choose to forgive for our own good not the other person. God says vengeance is His, He will repay. **"Bless those who persecute you; bless and do not curse. Rejoice with those who rejoice; mourn with those who mourn. Live in harmony with one another. Do not be proud, but be willing to associate with people of low position. Do not be conceited. Do not repay evil for evil. Be careful to do what is right in the eyes of everyone. If it is possible, as far as it depends on you, live at peace with everyone. Do not take revenge, my dear friends, but leave room for God's wrath, for it is written: "It is mine to avenge; I will repay," says the Lord. On the contrary: "If your enemy is hungry feed him; if he is thirsty, give him something to drink. In doing this, you will hip burning coals on his head. Do not be overcome by evil, but overcome evil with good."(Romans 12:14-21)**

In Christ we never lose; He already won the battle at the Cross. Believe and stand in the gap for your loved ones who have not come to know Christ yet. Remember you are not looking for victory, but you are fighting from a place of victory already won by Jesus Christ. God has *injected you* in your family to receive eternal *life through His Son Jesus Christ*, so that *you, by the authority given to you as a believer in Jesus name, can declare,* **"But as for me and my house, we will serve the LORD!"** Close every door of adversity and attack against your family and your spiritual progress. And in the name of Jesus by the authority given to you, resist and bind every spirit of oppression and heaviness.

Learn from God's Word to use every adverse situation and circumstance in your life to bring forth the fruit of Holiness rather than the fruit of sin and wickedness. And therefore, in defeating the enemy you turn these negative circles around by placing every situation under the blood of Jesus. ***The blood of Jesus Christ defeats everything!***

In Greek, the meaning of the word Salvation is, Sozo, it means to be redeemed, to be rescued, to be completely healed, to be made whole, to be subdued, to be saved and to be preserved. See the devil can't get you when you are really saved, but you have to know what your salvation means. It does not mean you are perfect, or that you never make mistakes, or even fall, rather it is because we are God's handiwork, created in Christ Jesus to do good works, which God prepared in advance for us to do. A ***righteous*** man falls seven times and ***gets up.*** God is going to fight your battles; He will make your wrongs right. If you stay on the high road and just keep being your best, you will see the hand of God at work in amazing ways. It may not happen overnight, but at the right time, in your due season, God will not only move wrong people out of the way, but He will also pay you back for injustice. Remember what God in the Scriptures says, how we are destroyed because of lack of knowledge. (See Hosea 4:6) It's not because we don't do right, but we don't do enough of what is right. **"All Scripture is inspired by God and profitable for teaching, for reproof, for correction, for training in righteousness; that the man of God may be adequate, equipped for every good work." (2 Timothy 3:16-17)** I cannot stress enough the importance of reading and the studying of the Word of God. It's in reading the

Scripture that we find out how God desires His children to live, and to partake of His promises.

My greatest desire is to continue having an intimate walk with My Heavenly Father. How good that Our God, Our Gracious Master calls all His children to serve as ambassadors in all that we do. How encouraging to know that every task we undertake as His servants is His work, even our smallest tasks! And in our prayer, we can put Him in our daily activities. God delights to see our faces and hear our voices, for He wants us to walk close to Him all day long, resting our hearts in the joy of who He is. **"Since, then, you have been raised with Christ, set your hearts on things above, where Christ is, seated at the right hand of God. Set your minds on things above, not on earthly things. For you died, and your life is now hidden with Christ in God. When Christ, who is your life, appears, then you will also appear with him in glory.**

**Put to death, therefore, whatever belongs to your earthly nature: sexual immorality, impurity, lust, evil desires and greed, which is idolatry. Because of these, the wrath of God is coming. You used to walk in these ways, in the life you once lived. But now you must also rid yourselves of all such things as these: anger, rage, malice, slander, and filthy language from your lips. Do not lie to each other, since you have taken off your old self with its practices and have put on the new self, which is being renewed in knowledge in the image of its Creator. Where there is no Gentile or Jew, circumcised or uncircumcised, barbarian or Scythian, slave or free, but Christ is all, and is in all." (Colossians 3:1-11)**

Author James P. Gills writes: "Please note that this is not what I do or don't do, before God it is strictly and solely: to be in Christ is to be righteous before God. (Rom.3:23-24) This enables us to affirm (without crossing our fingers) that in Christ- at the level of identity- the Christian is 100 percent righteous before God while at the same time recognizing the persistence of sin. If we don't speak in terms of two total states (100 percent righteous in Christ and 100 percent sinful in ourselves) corresponding to the coexistence of two times (the old age and the new creation) then the undeniable reality of ongoing sin leads to the qualification of our identity in Christ: the existence of some sin must mean that one is not totally righteous, *but in Christ.* This is acid at the very foundation of the peace we have with God on the other side of justification."

This good life that God expects those who love Him to live is impossible to live it out without salvation in Christ, who empowers the believer to live as an overcomer by the working power of the Holy Spirit in the believer, from glory to glory. **"Verily, Verily, I say unto you. He that believeth on me, the works that I do shall he do also; and greater *works* than these shall he do because I go unto my Father. And whatsoever ye shall ask in my name, that will I do, that the Father may be glorified in the Son. If ye love me, keep my commandments. And I will pray the Father, and he shall give you another Comforter that he may abide with you forever; *Even* the Spirit of truth: whom the world cannot receive, because it seeth him not, neither knoweth him: but ye know him; for he dwelleth with you, and shall be in you. I will not leave you comfortless: I will come to you. Yet a little while, and the world seeth me no more; but ye see me: because I live, ye shall live also. At that day ye shall know that I *am* in my Father, and ye in me, and I in you." (John 14:12-20)**

When we are going through very tough times and there is no relief in sight, we are prone to start looking for a way out. These escapist longings stem from self-pity and a sense of entitlement: We think we deserve better conditions than our current situation. But when we think this way, we are ignoring Gods' sovereignty over our life. Though your circumstances may indeed be painful and difficult, they are not worthless. So, muster the courage to say *yes* to your life, trusting God is in control and with you in your struggles. The Lord wants His children to come to Him with a courageous heart hoping in Him, and He will bless us in many ways. Moreover, He will multiply our small act of bravery: *I will strengthen your heart.* **"Be of good courage, and He shall strengthen your heart, all you who hope in the LORD."(Psalm 31:24 NKJV)**

I exult before the Lord because He is eternal and never-changing in His truth, in His attributes, and in His attitude toward me and all His loved ones. I'm so glad that His persistent tenderness binds my heart to Him forever…and that God who began a good work in me will carry it to completion until the day of Christ Jesus. God is utterly faithful and will finish what He set out to do. He will not abandon the work He begun. Praise the LORD!

**"Who is wise and understanding among you? Let them show it by their good life, by deeds done in the humility that comes from wisdom. But if you harbor bitter, envy and selfish ambition in your hearts, do not boast about it or deny the truth. Such "wisdom" does not come down from heaven but is earthly. Unspiritual, demonic. For where you have envy and selfish ambition, there you find disorder and every evil practice. But the wisdom that comes from heaven is first of all pure; then peace-loving, considerate, submissive, full of mercy and good fruit, impartial and sincere. Peacemakers who sow in peace reap a harvest of righteousness."(James 3:13-18)**

The devil however comes to deceive us; the battle indeed starts in our mind. As a man thinketh, so is he at last in action. So, if you want to change your life you have to change the way you think. Victimized by the lies of the devil through the battlefield of our mind, this too is a platform the devil uses to divert our thoughts to keep us bound and defeated. Our Spiritual blindness keeps us living defeated lives, blinded and unable to comprehend the life Christ died for us to live.

Christ didn't die for us to live as victims to our circumstances, but to overcome our circumstances by being alive to spiritual things and dead to carnal things. **"And they overcame him by the blood of the Lamb, and the word of their testimony; and they loved not their lives unto death. (Rev.12: 11)**

When it comes to failures, God says, **"I, even I, am he that blotteth out thy transgressions for mine own sake, and will not remember thy sins,"** (Isaiah 43:25). When it comes to wasted opportunities, God says, **"I will restore to you the years that the swarming locust has eaten,"** (Joel 2:25).

A wise man said, "If we do not learn from the past, we are doomed to repeat it." It's okay to look back and learn, but if you drive looking in the rearview mirror you'll end up in a ditch. Whether, good or bad, don't get stuck up in the past. **"Say not thou, 'What is the cause that the former days were better than these?' For thou dost not inquire wisely concerning this" (Ecc. 7:10).** If you are anxious about the future, recall God's faithfulness to you during the past year, count your blessings and name them one by one and you will be able to say, "Not a single one of all the good promises the Lord has given…was left unfulfilled; everything he(has) spoken came true," (Joshua 21:45 NLT). This is according to God's will for you. Cast your cares on the Sovereign God, the Blessed Controller of all things. God always wants, knows and is able to do what's best for His obedient trusting children. And He has promised to cause all things even things that are contrary to His ideal will- to fit into His pattern and His purpose for good for those who love Him. When we pray, we are to believe and expect God will grant us our request as He promised. (Mark 11:24)

Looking back Paul recalled times when there wasn't enough money in the kitty, and he had to go to work as a tentmaker in order to support his ministry. He could remember the hippings, the stonings, and the betrayals at the hands of those he trusted. But listen to what he says about it: **"Therefore having obtained help from God, to this day I stand,"(Act 26:22 NKJV).** We fail to receive help from God during difficult times because we don't really trust Him. Jeremiah felt the same way: **"Because of the Lord's great love we are not consumed, for his compassions never fail. They are new every morning; great is your faithfulness," (Lam 3:22-23).** We fail to receive help from God during difficult times because we don't really trust Him. No doubt, you failed God at some points, but did He ever fail you? No, that's why you are still here. God won't fail you now either, so trust Him. **"When I am afraid, I put my trust in you." (Psalm 56:3ESV)**

When adversity strikes, we either lash out angrily at God or become so focused on our problems that we forget His presence with us. An essential element of trusting the Lord is remembering

His promise. **"For I know the plans I have for you," declares the LORD. "Plans to prosper you and not to harm you, plans to give you a hope and a future. Then you will call on me and come and pray to me, and I will listen to you. You will seek and find me when you seek me with all your heart. I will be found by you." (Jeremiah 29:11-14a)** What a promise!

*A.B. Simpson wrote: "How often we trust each other, and only doubt our Lord. We take the words of mortals, yet distrust His Word; But, oh, what light and glory, would shine over all our days; if we always would remember, God means just what He says."*

## Submission to Governing Authorities

**"Let everyone be subject to the governing authorities, for there is no authority except that which God has established. The authorities that exist have been established by God. Consequently, whoever rebels against the authority is rebelling against what God has instituted, and those who do so will bring judgment on themselves."(Romans 13:1-2)**

We are not saved from death as much as we are saved through death. The old us, who try to get out of our situation by our own efforts, must be put to death. Otherwise, we might be tempted to take a little bit of the credit for our rescue. The Lord has rescued you, not by avoiding death, but by embracing it, taking the old you to the Cross with Him. Today, and every day, in Christ, you are made new. Praise the Lord!

When you choose not to resist your trials, but instead put your hope in God who is the Blessed Controller of all things, He is now, He will be throughout the future, and He always was. Then only can you see and be grateful that indeed all your past circumstances were permitted by God to make you see your need of Him, and to prepare your heart for His Word…to draw you to Himself, and to work out His good purposes for your life.

I know that all my days had God's touch of love and wisdom, whether or not I can yet fully see it. And so, I praise Him for the eternal glory these things are piling up for me as I choose to trust Him.

The tragedy of religion without power is that it leaves you ignorant of the incredible potential of prayer in any circumstance. Prayer moves God! And when God moves, people and situations change! Jesus told Peter, in Luke 22:31-32 that Satan had asked for him, that he may sift him as wheat. But that Jesus had prayed for Peter's faith not to fail him; Jesus then told Peter, when he returns to Him, to strengthen his brethren**. (Luke 22:31-32)** And God answered that prayer!

In spite of his denial of Christ, Peter ended up leading one of the greatest spiritual awakenings in history, and two of the books in the Bible are named after him. Only eternity will reveal the lives that have been salvaged and ministries restored through prayer. **"Whatever you ask for in prayer, believe that you have received it, and it will be yours," (Mark 11:24). While the Bible teaches self-worth, it also denounces self-interest. When Jesus was asked what the greatest commandment was, He said that we were to love God with all our hearts, and love others with the same concern that we show for ourselves.** (See **Mk 12:30-31)**

When we obsess over ourselves, we lose the meaning of life, which is to love and serve God, and love and serve our neighbors. Without commitment, our lives will lack meaning and purpose. After all, if nothing is worth dying for, then nothing is worth living for. Jesus taught that the only way to live abundantly is to die to self-interest and give yourself fully to God, and to those who need what God has given you. (See my first book, *Grace and Truth*: *Memoirs of Andeso*)

In the book of Romans, we learn that; **"The rulers hold no terror to those who do right, but for those who do wrong. Do you want to be free from fear of the one in authority? Then do what is right and you will be commended. For the one in authority is God's servant for your good. But if you do wrong,** be afraid for the rulers do not bear the sword for no reason. They are God's servants, agents of wrath to bring punishment on the wrongdoer. Therefore. It is necessary to submit to the authorities, not only because of punishment but also as a matter of conscience."(Romans 13:3-5)** Whether we get in trouble with the law and get the punishment we deserve, or for various reasons we experience life's most painful seasons, God uses all our trials and tribulations to remold and reshape us. God expects that in spite of what we think or feel when we get our eyes off Him, we should choose not to resist our trials as intruders, but to welcome them as friends. **"You have heard that it was said, 'Love your neighbor and hate your enemy.' But I tell you, love your enemies and pray for those who persecute you, that you may be children of your Father in heaven. He causes his sun to rise on the evil and the good, and sends rain on the righteous and the unrighteous. If you love those who love you, what reward will you get? Are not even the tax collectors doing that? And you if you greet only your own people, what are you doing more than others? Do not even the pagans do that?" (Mathew 5:43-47).**

"Enemies" are not always people but hindrances, shortcomings or all kinds of struggles we face in life. As believers in all these things, we are to have total trust in God, and to see each difficulty as an opportunity to see God work for our good. (1 Thessalonians 5:18) Thanking Him in advance, for in His time He will bring us to a place of abundance. Paul put it this way, **"Therefore I am well content with weaknesses, with insults, with distresses, with persecutions, with difficulties, for Christ's sake; for when I am weak, then I am strong." (2 Corinthians 12:10)**

God looks beyond our superficial desire for a trouble-free life; instead, He fulfils our deep-down desire to glorify Himself and to enjoy His warm fellowship as we become more Christlike.

**"In your struggle against sin, you have not yet resisted to the point of shedding your blood. And have you completely forgotten this word of encouragement that addresses you as a father addresses his son? It says, 'My Son, do not make light of the Lord's discipline, and do not lose heart when he rebukes**

**you, because he chastens everyone he accepts as his son.' "(Hebrews 12:4-6)**

I praise You God that "Jesus Christ is able to untangle all the snarls in my soul, to banish all our complexes, and to transform even our fixed habit patterns, no matter how deeply they are etched in your subconscious." (Corrie ten Boom)

No matter what you are struggling with today, even as a born again believer, rejoice because God is able to do far more than all you can ask or think, according to His power that raised Jesus from the dead! Christ came to set the captives free. Speak God's Word in your situation until you see the change you desire take place. **"Either make the tree good, and his fruit good; or else make the tree corrupt, and his fruit corrupt: for the tree is known by his fruit. O generation of vipers, how can ye, being evil, speak good things? For out of the abundance off the heart the mouth speaketh." (Matthew 12:33-34)**

"The words of our mouth give expression to what we think, feel and want. Our words reveal what our hearts contain and are ultimately a result of who we believe we are. What does Jesus mean by "abundance" in this verse? He means "the surplus." It is the buildup and overflow of whatever is in abundance in your heart. What is in you will eventually come out! You can't confront what you don't identify.

God will reveal the negative cycles of generational cursing in our lives, so that they may be overturned with the blessing of Abraham. God's revelation is never a condemnation…He wants us to confront what He identifies in our life! God never identifies an area we have to change without giving us the tools to confront these areas in His Word.

We are to recognize, admit to God the negative confessions we've made about ourselves, and others, and repent of it. It's in using the One and Only name JESUS that we revoke…unsay or cancel negative the negative confessions. And then we replace our wrong confession with what God says about us, as His children.

God's Word says: *1.You are fearfully and wonderfully made*. **Ps.139:14.** *2. You are God's workmanship created in Christ*

*Jesus.* **Eph.2:10.** *3. You are victorious.* **Rev. 21:7.** *4. You are established to the end.* **1 Cor. 1:18.** *5. You are called by God.* **2 Timothy 1:9.** *6. You are more than a conqueror.* **Rom. 8:37.** *7. You are an ambassador for Christ.* **2 Cor. 5:20.** *8. You are beloved of God.* **1 Thess.1:4.** *9. You are the joint heir.* **Rom. 8:17.** *10. You will be overtaken with blessings.* **Deut. 28:2.** *11. You are complete in Christ.* **Col.2:10.** *12. You are firmly rooted, built up, and strengthened in faith.* **Col.2:7.** *13. You will always triumph.* **2 Cor. 2:14.**

Which myth do you need to "root out" and replace with God's truth? Which scripture will you stand on this week? There is a redeeming quality to being forgiven-conscious, as opposed to being conscious of your failings, sins and mistakes. When you are forgiveness-conscious and see your failings on the Cross of Jesus, you receive power to break out of irritability, impatience, and short temperedness with others. You receive power to break out of your eating disorders, addictions, and anxieties!

When you realize that we don't deserve God's forgiveness and grace, yet He gives it to us anyway. This revelation of His unmerited favor changes us from within. It dissolves the knots of anger, insecurities and impatience in us that has built up over the years and frees us to enjoy God's love and to show it to others. The key, therefore, is to receive His grace as unmerited favor and believe that same unmerited favor is what transforms you. Grace produces divine empowerment, but in and of itself, the essence of grace is Gods undeserved, unmerited, and unearned favor. When you are in your most undeserving state? When you have failed. Unmerited favor means that when you have failed and are in your most undeserving state, you can receive Jesus' favor, blessings, love and perfect acceptance in your life.

## "Fessing Up"

It's one thing to desire truth, but to pursue it you must: **"Put off your old self...and...put on the new self, created to be like God,"(Ephesians 4:24).** One author writes: "We must be willing to have the conversations our 'old self' would have avoided...It's not easy...it requires heavy doses of humility and accepting that we're going to be uncomfortable...No matter how uncomfortable it is...the truth sets us free."

But life can take you to places you never thought you'd go or do things you never ever thought you would do; the flesh is stubborn and can only be overcome by the Spirit of God.

When we are at the end of our rope, when we no longer have hope for ourselves, that's when we run to God for mercy, for in Jesus we have everything we need. When my religious cards that glory built collapsed, when I had encountered pain and suffering. When suddenly, my mask came off, and my glory road reached the end, I was at the place where if I had to find any help or comfort, it had to come from a place out of myself; in Christ alone I found my rest, He is my solid rock. Call on Him; your life will be transformed.

I thank God for His sovereignty over the broad events of my life and over the details. With God, nothing is accidental, and neither is anything incidental, and no experience is wasted. He holds in His own power, my breath of life and all my destiny. And every trial that God allows to happen is a platform on which He has revealed Himself, and has shown me His love and power, both to me and others looking on. God's everlasting love strengthened me in my time of weakness and has definitely helped me to move into the future non-defensively, trusting Him Who knows and sees the beginning from the end. My times are in His hands.

**"But what can I say? He has spoken to me, and he himself has done this. I will walk humbly all my years because of this anguish of my soul. Lord, by such things people live; and my spirit finds life in them too. You restored me to health and let me live. Surely it was for my benefit that I suffered such anguish. In your love you kept me from the pit of destruction; you have put all my sin behind your back. For the grave cannot praise you, death cannot sing your praise, those who go down to the pit cannot hope for your faithfulness. The**

living, the living-they praise you, as I am doing today; parents tell their children about your faithfulness." (Isaiah 39:15-19)**

## A Hiding Place

Let God's grace dethrone your hurt and your fears. Anxiety still comes for certain, and trouble can populate your world, but these things don't control it, if you can only hide God's Word in your heart and take refuge, it's a hiding place! And healing comes. **"Whoever dwells in the shelter of the Most High will rest in the shadow of the Almighty. I will say of the LORD, 'He is my refuge and my fortress, my God, in whom I trust.' " (Ps.91:1-2)** God promises He will commanded His angels concerning you to guard you in all your ways and to meet your needs in His way at the right time. During times when I have felt utter despair, defeated, hopeless and a failure, when I've been trampled on, talked about for my troubled life, God's been there with me wiping my tears, helping me from strength-to-strength. He always was there to teach me and kept pointing me to Jesus Christ as the answer to my hang-ups, and my only Source who meets my deepest needs. Jesus Christ is my wonderful counsellor and mighty in power, the only one that heals from the inside out. **"I, the LORD your God, will hold your right hand, saying to you, 'Fear not, I will help you.' " (Isaiah 41:13)**

I've often asked myself how can one person have so many troubles? **"For this thing I besought the Lord thrice, that it might depart from me. And he said unto me, 'My grace is sufficient for thee: for my strength is made perfect in weakness.' Most gladly therefore will I rather glory in my infirmities, that the power of Christ may rest upon me," (2 Corinthians 12:8-9).** In my feelings of betrayal, rejection and failure, in my seemingly state of hopelessness and defeat...the Lord was right there with me, waiting, guiding, comforting me, and causing me not to lose my mind. **"Do not be afraid of those who kill the body but cannot kill the soul. Rather, be afraid of the One who can destroy both soul and body in hell. Are not two sparrows sold for a penny? Yet not one of them will fall to**

**the ground outside your Father's care. And even the very hairs of your head are all numbered. So don't be afraid; you are worth more than many sparrows,"(Mathew 10:28-31).**

God expects us to defeat our circumstances, and not the other way around. He expects us to grow in holiness so that we will not dishonor His name, that we will be a good advertisement for the Gospel. He is a God of peace and well-being who is committed to making us holy, day-by-day, giving us grace to cooperate with the Holy Spirit. He is faithful and He will continue His work in us until the day when He brings us faultless into His glorious presence, with unspeakable joy. God's work is no less profound than resurrection. He creates life out of death, something out of nothing, and righteousness out of sin. And He has done that for you and me. There's no doubt, the why questions of suffering are utterly perplexing.

And as we search the Scriptures and consider stories such as Job's, we are tempted to see those as worst-case scenarios designed to help us get our heads straight in relation to our comparatively small "first world problems." We medicate, we minimize; we moralize. We develop theories to explain what is happening to us. While they may temporarily help us categorize and compartmentalize our thoughts and feelings, when true suffering comes, all our speculations fall flat.

Since no one alive can see the beginning from the end, from the divine vantage point, we're left stranded in a prison of inscrutability. And sadly, we often prefer our confinement to the disorienting possibility that *our suffering is actually ordained, that God is involved in it. In fact, the Cross tells us that He does so (and has done so) through suffering, not to despite it.*

Justin Holcomb puts it this way in his book *On the Grace of God: Grace is available because Jesus went through the valley of the shadow of death and rose from the death. The gospel engages our life with all its pain, shame, rejection, our blindness, sin, and death. So now, to your pain, the gospel says, "You will be healed."*

*Beauty for Ashes*

    The good news of suffering is that it brings us to the end of ourselves. God uses our life circumstances, other people, family members and friends, each disturbing or humbling situation in our lives to expose our weaknesses and to perfect our faith, which prepares our hearts for the fresh new growth in godliness that God desires to see in His children. How grateful I am of the Holy Spirit of wisdom and understanding, He guides us, brings counsel and strengthens those who lean on Him.

# CHAPTER THIRTEEN

## God Is A Restorer

It is heartbreaking and challenging for a parent when a child turns their back on their faith in Christ, and instead turns to a different religion. When you've been through some things like I've been, and when you've experienced abuse, been broken hearted, broken the law yourself... and then you've experienced the grace of God, you know there is no other hope out there, but the saving grace of God Nothing whatsoever can separate you and me from the love of God! **"Neither height nor depth, not anything else in all creation, will be able to separate us from the love of God that is in Christ Jesus our Lord."(Romans 8:39)**

You tend to hold your children just a little tighter, fear can take over, you beat yourself up because you've not been a perfect parent and they have watched you make some blunders in life, and we all have because there is no perfect parent, none whatsoever. Boy the devil can take you to task if you have not learnt to surrender all things, good and bad, past present and future in the Maker of all mankind, the Almighty God! The devil will "take that and run with it...causing you to remain fearful, worried and stressed out. I've walked that road already. This self-centeredness only promotes self-condemnation, and in His evil and conniving ways, the accusations will keep on coming to bring depression...the devil will use your past to tear you down. If you don't know that Christ died for your past, present and future sins...the devil will drag you through the mud. Know who you are in Christ, *know* the Word of God. Even though you live in a world where trouble is inescapable, you can be of good cheer because He has overcome the world! **"These things I have spoken to you, that in Me you may have peace. In the world you will have tribulations; but be of good cheer, I have overcome the world." (John 16:33 NKJV)**

Remember, we were designed to embrace God and others, but instead we are now consumed with ourselves. The Gospel causes us to look up to Christ and what He did, and outward to our neighbors and what they need, not inward to ourselves and only what we need. There's nothing about the Gospel that fixes eyes on me. Any version of Christianity therefore that encourages you to think mostly about you is detrimental to your faith-whether it's your failures or your successes, your good works or your bad works, your strength or your weaknesses, your obedience or your disobedience. The irony, of course, is that you and I are renewed inwardly to the degree that we focus not on inward renewal but upward worship and outward service. The more you see that the Gospel isn't about you, the more spiritual *you* will become.

That's why I thank God that I can move into the future non-defensively, with hands outstretched to whatever lies ahead, for I know He holds the future and He will always be with me, even to my old age…and through eternity. **"There is none like Thee, O Lord; Thou art great, and great is Thy name in might,"(Jeremiah 10:6).** I know that my prayers are not in vain and God's Word will not return to Him void. Every prayer will be answered, in His time and manner. God is faithful. He does not change; He is the same yesterday, today and forever. You have to have faith, the God who delivered you will deliver your loved ones. God is able to draw them back. Your total trust in God will move your mountain. Dig your heels in the Word and know He's walking with you all the way, thanking Him for the Holy Spirit- the Spirit of wisdom and understanding, the Spirit of counsel and strength. He enables us to give thanks for all things always at all times.

The Holy Spirit is authorized to act on God's Word when *you* begin to say what God has said. So, get into God's Word and begin to stand on it. Get God's Word into you and start speaking it over your situation and over your children and those you love as the Spirit of God leads you. And when you learn to listen with your heart, you'll hear God's comforting word of hope. In times like those it's loving our children without judging and criticizing that will bring them around. At some point you have to get over the bothersome and hear what the Spirit of God is saying to *you* as you stand in the gap for those you love.

We all know that we are expected to grow up. We've heard it all our lives, even from the Bible. Colossians 1, Ephesians 4, and 1 Corinthians 3 all ask us to grow up. The pressing question is how. Listen to Jesus: **"The kingdom of God is as if someone would scatter seed on the ground, and would sleep and rise night and day, and the seed would sprout and grow, he does not know how," (Mark 4:26-27 NRSV).** God gives growth. We work the soil, but it is God alone who gives the growth. We think Christian growth is all about willpower. But the good and relieving news is that Christian growth is not about our willpower in the same way that planted seed do not grow themselves. Christian growth is all about grace- the grace of a Father who works in us to will and to work for His good pleasure.

Although, the Law breaks even the hardest of hearts, exposes us and offers no fixes, ***grace*** exonerates us and heals our brokenness. It is when we can look ourselves in the mirror and be honest about what we see – our failings, sins, and shortcomings- that we can begin to live our lives with some measure of freedom. But as long as we look into that mirror and tell ourselves that glory is possible, we'll be a nervous wreck. We'll be terrified of exposure, of failure, of being outed as frauds. Once we face our flaws, we find that our freedom is so much better. Our errors, our embarrassing falls, and our public disgraces have been given to a substitute. His perfect score has been given to us. We now live secure in the knowledge that when the Judge regards us, He sees only His blameless Son Jesus Christ. Fortunately, our faults can never come back to us. All Glory to the Almighty God who has loved us with an everlasting love!

### Prayer

Do you ever wonder why God chose to link His actions with our praying? Why did He decide that our prayers would cause Him to accomplish certain things or expand what He does?

And that by not praying, we would limit Him? Could He not have carried out His purposes far more efficiently without us? Yet, He has established the prayers of His people as a powerful influence on how and when He meets our material, emotional and spiritual needs, and the needs of others throughout the world.

I would like to encourage those who have children, relatives or even friends who have gotten off course that although things may look impossible, but if you'll stay in faith, everything God promised in His Word will come to fulfillment. God is going to finish what He started. You will see them reconciled to the Lord. Whatever the situation, tarry in prayer, prayers of thanksgiving, praise and worship for what Christ has already accomplished on our behalf. No one can stop Him from fulfilling His promises. Bad breaks can't stop it; sickness can't stop it. Death can't even stop it. In other words, you will not go to your grave without fulfilling your God ordained destiny, unless *you* choose to forfeit it.

The Scripture in the book of Ephesians confirms our lifelong everlasting position and status in Christ, our generational blessing of our identity in Him. **(Ephesians 1:4-12)** Many of our fears come from our failing to grasp our position and status in Christ. We are overloaded with guilty feelings and burdened with a poor self-image that leads to fear of failure, rejection and other qualms.

When you are saved, you are placed into union with Jesus Christ. You are one with Him, united in death, burial and resurrection. You are His adopted child, placed into *His forever family*. Who are you in Christ? Are there events or issues in life that, like David, Moses or Saul, make you feel afraid? What can you do in those situations by faith in Christ? Are there any aspects of your identity in Christ that the enemy seems to challenge the most? Notice David's response to fear in Psalm 56:3, "When I am afraid, I put my trust in you." David did not conceal his worry before God. Isn't it futile to conceal our true feelings before an omniscient God anyway?

You are not under condemnation. (Romans 8:1) You are completely accepted by Christ despite inconsistent behavior.

(Eph.1:3-4) God never accuses you or berates you. (Romans 8:31-39) You can do all things through Christ according to (Philippians 4:13). You have a new identity in Christ!

We sometimes think we are less spiritual for letting God, or others, know about our fears. That concern is not a Biblical one, for many of the greatest men and women of the Scriptures were gripped by various sorts of fears and did not hide them from God. Many of the Psalms were penned by the trembling hand of David, who lived in the shadows of fear for many years while on the run from Saul. Our lives are the paper that God writes on. Many sermons will be borne out of the furnace of affliction. People are going to watch you go through it, and if it weren't for watching your story of overcoming generational curses, they would have no answers or point of reference. Your life is the Bible that others are reading!

The entire fulfillment of your destiny hinges on the way you choose to deal with life's troubles, trials and times of transition. When you reach a "breaking point," will you outlast the adversity, or will it outlast you? Will you keep going around the mountain, or will you break the chain and pass the test? THIS is how your generational patterns of curses are broken. You break the circle of dysfunction and do things GOD'S WAY. You shall be an overcomer, because of Jesus Christ!

The way you choose to deal with your trial depends on where you go next. Calm faith and trust in God receive deliverance before it ever appears. Jesus feels our griefs and our sorrows; He has been touched with the feelings of our weaknesses. (Heb.4:15) He understands the things that hurt us and is capable of empathizing completely with our current conditions and past wounding. Many of us have been through disastrous, life-shattering episodes that changed everything. But God doesn't want us to hurt; He wants to heal every place and restore us completely!

God is all-powerful, and there's none like Him. Glory to His name! Nothing is beyond His influence or control, not your wayward son or daughter, their self-defeating habits, the unrelenting sickness or life's challenges. **"Though the LORD is exalted, he looks kindly on the lowly; though lofty, he sees them from afar. Though I walk in the midst of trouble, you preserve my life. You stretch out your hand against the anger of my foes; with your right hand you save me. The LORD will vindicate me; your love LORD, endures forever—do not abandon the works of your hands."(Psalm 138:6-8)**

Your reputation lies in the truth that you have been saved and belong to God, that you have been equipped in Christ to face any situation of life and overcome it, and that you are lovable because Christ first loved you. You can't give up now until you see God's promise come to pass, in Joshua's words, *"But as for me and my house, we will serve the Lord."* Let God do His part, the battle is His. You be you, and do your part, that is to trust and to obey Him. **"I will praise thee; for I am fearfully made: marvelous are thy works; and my soul knoweth right well." (Psalm139:14)**

God created us to be His loved ones, His family with whom He can share a relationship of mutual enjoyment. God is a personal God who values loving relationships more than anything else in all the universe. Even when we don't pray, God still holds together every molecule in our bodies; He's still the source of every good thing. But prayer keeps us aware of Him as our Source and opens our lives to receive His greater bounty. So, let us along with prayer, invest in His written Word because without faith it's impossible to please God. And faith cometh by hearing and hearing the word of God. Never forget what God has done for you and me at the Cross; He has loved us with an everlasting love. **"The LORD is compassionate and gracious, slow to anger and abounding in love. He will not always accuse, nor will he harbor his anger forever; he does not treat us as our sins deserve or repay us according to our iniquities. For as high as the heavens are above the earth, so great is his love for those who fear him; as far as the east is from the west, so far has he removed our transgressions from us.(Psalm 103:8-12)**

When we sin and confess our transgressions, God is just to forgive us. We have to be humble enough, to acknowledge our part and forgive others and ourselves and then turn to the Lord for forgiveness. None of us are perfect and we will never ever be, not one person, only Jesus Christ is perfect. The Holy Spirit convicts us to bring transformation, but as believers we are not condemned and therefore, we should not condemn ourselves, instead we are to delight ourselves in the Lord. We are the righteousness of God in Christ.

I will forever exult in God's marvelous grace- in His favor and blessings which I do not deserve-for He has raised me with Christ and seated me with Him in the heavenly realm, far above any conceivable command, authority, power, or control. But how grateful I am that He has linked me to the greatest possible purposes, the highest of all reasons for living: to know and to love Him and to show His love to other people…to glorify Him, to enjoy Him now and forever. What an honor!

## Our Worship, Praise and Thanksgiving

I thank God that what's impossible with man is possible with God! Through praise you give God something no one else in Heaven or Earth can give, the love and adoration of your heart. He chose you before He created the Earth. He designed you as a unique original, so that you would be a special person unlike any other. He made you for Himself. And He has made plans for an intimate relationship with you throughout all eternity. Such a God is not indifferent to your response to Him. Your praise makes Him glad. Your neglect grieves Him. Did you know that praise can help you fulfill your destiny, your chief purpose in this life and the next? Those who love Him will praise and worship Him in Spirit and in truth.

**The Westminster Catechism condenses volumes of scriptural truth when it says:**

**"The chief end of man is to glorify God and to enjoy Him forever. Through worship, praise, and thanksgiving you minister directly to God, who seeks for people to worship Him. Here lies the most compelling reason for praise. God does not**

enjoy your praise because He's conceited and loves the limelight. He enjoys it because praise is an indispensable part of relating to him, the Creator and Supreme ruler who is exalted high above all. God is holy and infinite and all powerful, and you and I are specks in a vast universe who receive from Him life and breath and all things. So worship, praise, and thanksgiving bring needed realism into our fellowship with Him. They make possible a true, deep, mutually satisfying relationship." So, immerse yourself in praise and worship your Creator. You'll discover anew your Father's understanding, His deep and abiding compassion for you…the strength of His Word to meet your deepest longings and needs.

### How can We Obey if we don't know?

Jesus said that those who love Him *will* obey His commandments. Not "you'd better." You *will.* He's not simply asking you to; He's not just telling you to. He's promising that *you will.* When we worry, and look up to Heaven and ask, "Lord do you love me?" Jesus says, "Look to the Cross. It is proof I love you."

What happens when unprepared Christians are plunged into darkness by the trials of life? They begin to question what's happening. Everything was going well; all they could see ahead was fair weather. If they have not spent time in God's Word or have not been taught to trust God regardless of what they see or feel, they will get discouraged, sometimes backslide, and sometimes even blame God and get swallowed up in bitterness. Paul writes to Timothy, **"Study and be eager and do your utmost to present yourself to God approved (tested by trial), a workman who has no cause to be ashamed, correctly analyzing and accurately driving the Word of Truth. (2 Timothy 2:15)PG.47**

Life has its ways of interrupting even the most perfectly laid out human plans with God out of the equation. What then? Faith in God, His word, trusting in Him and walking in obedience needs to be our life of worship before God. All other ground is sinking sand.

The Author Tullian Tchividjian writes: "Justification and sanctification are both God's work, and while they can and must be distinguished, the Bible won't let us separate them. Both are gifts of our union with Christ and, within this double blessing, justification is the root of sanctification, and sanctification is the fruit of justification. Moralism happens when we separate the fruit from the root. When we understand that everything between God and us has been fully and finally made right, that Christians live their lives under a banner that reads, 'It is finished, we necessarily turn away from ourselves and turn toward our neighbor. Forever freed from our need to pay God back or secure God's love and acceptance, we are now free to serve others. I can now actively spend my life giving instead of taking, going to the back instead of angling for the front, sacrificing myself for others instead of sacrificing others for myself."

Total trust in God through Jesus Christ is the answer to mankind's' struggles, and to believe and to embrace what Christ has accomplished on the Cross is spiritual awakening in our journey through life. Your medical record may say there's no way you will get well, it may look like you may never get a financial breakthrough in life, or you may be side-blinded by the fact that your children will never be reconciled to the LORD to His glory, that job you've been trusting the LORD for may never come, the dwindling business looks like you might have to give up, the unaffordable college tuition, the poor economy ... and the list goes on.

The thing is, when God puts a promise in your heart, you have to come to the place where you believe in that promise so strongly no one can talk you out of it. It doesn't mean fear, worry, anxiety or depression won't attack you, but you have to have enough Word in you to drive out fear, to drive out anxiety and to drive out the discouraging voice of the enemy. **"For the Word of God is alive and active. Sharper than any two-edged sword, it penetrates even to dividing soul and spirit, joints and marrow; it judges the thoughts and attitudes of the heart. Nothing in all creation is hidden from God's sight. Everything is uncovered**

**and laid bare before the eyes of him to whom we must give account."(Hebrews 4:12-13)**

To instill the Word of God in your heart, changes you and you begin to have the mind of Christ and think the thoughts of the Messiah! The Bible is called the Living Word for a reason, the word of God changes lives, don't take it lightly you will be amazed! I just can't say it enough. (See **2 Timothy 3:16-17**) God cared enough to communicate with us in this clear, unchanging, always-accessible way, so that His thoughts are always available at all times to refresh and nourish and teach us.

What a privilege to store God's Word in my heart where He can use it at any moment to bless me, guide me…and keep me from sinning against Him…and to be a storehouse of inspired words that the Spirit can bring to my mind to help me and others. It's in knowing the Word of God that I discovered His will for me and His patterns for living and serving Him. Don't think you were cheated out of life and use it as an excuse to be bitter. That attitude will only keep the blessings of God from entering your life. God never promised life would be fair. He did promise that if you stay in faith, He would take what is meant for your harm and use it to your advantage.

Nothing happens to you that surprises God, neither has any incident that has happened in your life taken God by surprise and caught Him off guard. I had to get over the painful past, within that I had to stop reliving all the hurt and move forward…only then did I come to the new beginning God had in store for me. I'm grateful to the Holy Spirit for inspiring the Word of God, and how He uses it to enlighten and guide me, and to change me more and more into Christ's image from one degree of glory to another.

## A Made-up Mind

This is what the Apostle Paul did. He had a made up mind. He said, **"None of these things moves me,"(Acts 20:24). What things? Circumstances that looked impossible, or people saying it will never happen, or negative or discouraging thoughts**. His attitude was: "It doesn't change my mind. *I'm not moved by what I see. I am moved by what I know. And I know if God is for me who dares be against me? I know God's promises are yes and amen. I know God has the last say."* That is unshakable faith, but we have to know the Word of God and believe what it says. **"The heart of the discerning acquires knowledge, for the ears of the wise seek it out,"(Proverbs 18:15).** It does not mean that we don't respect and honor those trying to help us, but we know God can do what medical science cannot do. I know God made my body. Doctors can treat me, but only God can heal me." And this is what the LORD says: **"Cursed is the one who trusts in man, who draws strength from mere flesh and whose heart turns away from the LORD. That person will be like a bush in the wastelands; they will not see prosperity when it comes. They will dwell in the parched places of the desert, in a salt land where no one lives."** We must be saved, nothing can buy you favor with God, not silver nor gold, only by the spotless precious blood of Jesus Christ, the Son of God, are we saved. Jesus never separates Himself from the Word.

**Radical Love!**

Where does it all begin? Without salvation in Jesus' Name, no man shall see God! **"And we have seen and do testify that the Father sent the Son to be the Savior of the world. Whosoever shall confess that Jesus is the Son of God, God dwelleth in him, and he in God. And we have known and believed the love that God hath for us. God is love; and he that dwelleth in love dwelleth in God, and God in Him. Herein is our love made perfect, that we have boldness in the day of judgement: because as he is so are, we in this world. There is no fear in love: because fear hath torment. He that feareth is**

**not perfect in love. We love him, because he first loved us."(1 John 4-19)**

Unless you hear God's voice speaking to you from the Scriptures, you will remain in that natural, darkened state of being. Jesus said, **"The words I speak to you are spirit, and they are life," (John 6:63)**. Jesus told Nicodemus, a religious teacher of the Jews, that his education would not save him. He explained that unless he became born again by the Spirit, he would never see the kingdom of God. (See **John 3**)

Only in that supernatural experience of *accepting Christ as your Savior* and being born again will you receive a supernatural change of your desires and motivations. Coming to know the wonderful forgiveness and life of Christ within you births desires to please God, and to live in devotion to Jesus. Until that happens, the Bible will not make sense to you. The Bible calls you to love the Savior as your first affection and your portion in life. But you will not serve God and sacrifice yourself to honor Him without first being given a new heart by accepting Christ as your personal Savior.

"The natural man who views the universe as a clutch of impersonal forces also views Jesus as merely a historical figure. The natural man has no conception of the present and living Christ walking beside the believer, as He did with the disciples on the road to Emmaus. The Bible says, **"Taste and see that the LORD is good," (Psalm 34:8),** but the unbeliever does not taste, and he cannot see. His completely natural state leaves him focused on the immediate and apparent, rather than on the eternal.

For us to depart from such blindness and to enter into a living faith in Christ, we must believe He is risen and waiting in Heaven to welcome us. This hope must stir us to live our lives here in the light of eternity. To have true peace, we must believe that we are forgiven and delivered from the judgment of hell. Our total redemption is accomplished by the blood of Jesus shed for us at Calvary. We can look into the face of death and know that we are **"...more than conquerors through Him who loved us." (Romans 8:37)**

## God Will Never Forsake You

"**My God, why have You forsaken Me?**"(**Psalm 22:1**) And after the darkness, three quick words. First, a plea: "**I thirst!**"(**John 19:28**), revealing the human side of our Lord. And then the *proclamation:* "**It is finished!**"(**John 19:30**).

"My God…why have You forsaken Me?" Many people know all too well the raw heartbreak that comes with being forsaken. Countless children who have been abandoned by fathers or mothers live for years in the dark shadow of being forsaken. But God will never forsake His own people. Did He forsake Shadrach, Meshack, and Abed-Nego in a fiery furnace (Daniel 3) or Daniel in a lions' den (Daniel 6)? No! Then why this loud cry, this strange question from the dry, parched lips of our Lord as He hung from the Cross.

We are reminded in Habakkuk 1:3 that God the Father is so holy that He cannot even look upon sin. This truth is why, on the Cross, the words of **Isaiah 53:6** became reality; "**All we like sheep have gone astray…and the LORD has laid on Him [Christ] the iniquity of us all.**" The apostle Paul put it like this: "**[God] made [Jesus] who knew no sin to be sin for us, that we might become the righteousness of God in Him,**" (**2 Corinthians 5:21**). On the Cross, Jesus took our sin in His own body, suffering shame, hurt, humiliation, pain, agony and death—the consequences that we deserved; God the Father could not look upon the sin His Son was bearing, so He turned away. Darkness enveloped the Earth as Jesus fought our battle with Satan on the Cross. His words: *"My God, why have You forsaken Me?"* come directly from: ***Psalm 22:1,*** as though Jesus, quoting this prophecy, was saying**, *"I will endure this separation so that any and all who come to Me will never have to be separated from God and will never experience the pain of being forsaken by their heavenly Father…"*** And that is you and me.

Is it any wonder the Bible says, "Thanks be to God for His indescribable gift! (2 Corinthians 9:15)? On the Cross, instead of giving up, our Lord reached up. In place of giving in, He reached in. And in place of giving out, He reached out. What a Savior. And yes, "Thanks be to God for His indescribable gift!"

Have you ever had a chance to invite Jesus into your heart? It is the most important decision you will ever make. Below, I have written a prayer of salvation. (You might confess aloud with your mouth and heart believing as you recite the words below.)

### *Salvation Prayer*

*Father it is written in Your Word that if I confess with my mouth that Jesus is Lord and believe in my heart that you have raised Him from the dead, I will be saved. Therefore, Father, I confess that Jesus is my Lord. I receive Jesus Christ as my Lord and Savior and make Him Lord of my life right now. I renounce my past life with Satan and close the door to any of his devices.*

*I am a new creation in Christ Jesus. I have a new life in Christ, old things have passed away.*

*I thank you for forgiving me of all my sins by the blood of Jesus. I am saved and justified by faith, Jesus became sin that I might be the righteousness of God.*

*I am now your child, God. I have been born again and am made new in Christ Jesus. Holy Spirit, help me to live the life that God has for me.*

If you said this prayer and meant every word, welcome to the Kingdom of God! You just got born-again. Please look for and join a good church, invest in reading the Word of God daily and if possible, join a small group in your new church that can help you grow, tell others about your new faith in Christ Jesus as your Lord and Savior. **"Whosoever therefore shall confess me before men, him will I also confess before my Father which is in heaven. But whosoever shall deny me before men, him will l also deny before my Father which is in heaven." (Mathew 10:32-33)**

# CHAPTER FOURTEEN

## The Gospel

**The Gospel is Foolishness to those who are perishing**

"For the message of the Cross is foolishness to those who are perishing, but to us who are being saved it is the power of God. For it is written: **"I will destroy the wisdom of the wise; the intelligence of the intelligent I will frustrate. Where is the wise person? Where is the teacher of the law? Where is the philosopher of this age? For since in the wisdom of God the world through its wisdom did not know him, God was pleased through the foolishness of what was preached to save those who believe. Jews demand signs and Greeks look for wisdom, but we preach Christ crucified: a stumbling block to Jews and foolishness to Gentiles. But to those whom God has** *called*, **both Jews and Greeks, Christ the power of God and the wisdom of God. For the foolishness of God is wiser than human wisdom, and the weakness of God is stronger than human srength.**

**Brothers and sisters, think of what you were when you were called. Not many of you were wise by human standards; not many were influential; not many were of noble birth. But God chose the weak things of the world to shame the strong. God chose the lowly things of the world to shame the wise; and the despised things—and the things that are not—to nullify— the things that are, so that** *no one may boast before Him.* **It is because of him that you are in Christ Jesus, who has become for us wisdom from God—that is, our righteousness, holiness and redemption."** Therefore, as it is written: **"Let the one who boasts boast in the Lord."**(1 Cor. 1:18-31)

The Bible makes it clear that the power that saves even the worst rule-breaking sinner is the Gospel (Rom.1:16), and not the Law (Rom. 7:13-24). As if that weren't enough, there's another reason why preaching the Gospel of free grace is both necessary and effective, even at a time when moral laxity reigns supreme: Moralism is what most people outside the church think Christianity is all about. Unbelievers generally think the message of the church is "Behave!"

**"People believe that God is most interested in people becoming good instead of people coming to terms with how bad they really are so they'll fix their eyes on Christ, 'the author and perfecter of faith," (Heb.12:2 NASB)**. From a human standpoint, this is precisely why many people outside the church reject Christianity and why many people inside the church conk out: they're just not good enough to get it done over the long haul.

Many of us quickly forget that Jesus Christ died on the Cross to pay the full penalty for all our sins and make us acceptable to God. And we receive these benefits by faith alone; what Jesus did was enough. Now we do not pray in our own name or worth ("Lord, You should answer my prayers because I've been reading my Bible and living a good life." Instead, we approach Him solely in His name trusting in Who He is and what He Alone has done. Our attitude should be that of gratitude; "Thank You, Lord Jesus, that as a 'Christ-follower' I am called by Your noble and wonderful name. By your undeserved favor, I have been made a member of your royal family. Now I can approach You boldly, in Your merits alone. I expect You to answer my prayers because I come in Your name, concerned about what You want. What a privilege!"

Paul was accused on more than one occasion of preaching lawlessness and in Romans 6, he answers the assumption that preaching grace produces licentiousness, not by backing off of the Gospel, but by preaching the Gospel even more. Imagine it would have been tempting for Paul to put the brakes on grace and give the Law in this passage, but instead he gives more grace. Paul knows that licentious people aren't those who believe the Gospel of God's free grace too much, but too little."

The truth is that when we are in the throes of consequences for foolish things we do, our only hope is to remember that **"...there is therefore now no condemnation for those who are in Christ Jesus," (Romans 8:1 ESV).** In fact, the kind of suffering that comes from the consequences of sin is like a bushfire that burns away every thread of hope we have in ourselves and leaves only the thread of divine grace—a thread that will never break no matter how foolish we may be.

### *The Lord is not slack*

"Knowing this first, that there shall come in the last days scoffers, walking after their own lusts. And saying, where is the promise of his coming? For since the fathers fell asleep, all things continue as *they were* from the beginning of the creation. But the heavens and the earth, which are now, by the same word are kept in store, reserved unto fire against the Day of Judgment and perdition of ungodly men. For this they willingly are ignorant of, that by the word of God the heavens were of old, and the earth standing out of the water and in the water: Whereby the world that then was, being overflowed with water perished. But the heavens and the earth, which are now, by the same Word are kept in store, reserved unto fire against the day of judgment and perdition of ungodly men.(2 Peter 3:3-7)

### The Second Death

Only those who truly submitted to God and successfully resisted Satan throughout their lives will take part in this glorious future. Notice: **"He that *overcomes* shall INHERIT ALL THINGS; and I will be his God, and he shall be My son. But the fearful, and unbelieving, and the abominable, and murderers, and whoremongers, and sorcerers, and idolaters, and all lairs, shall have their part in the lake of which burns with fire and brimstone: which is the second death," (Rev.21:7-8).** Could you be one who INHERITS ALL THINGS in God's Kingdom?

Death is human kind's common denominator; death knocks on the door of the wealthiest billionaire and the poorest of peasants and sends them both to stand before the Judge of the Universe. No wonder Amos thundered out the warning, **"Prepare to meet your God," (Amos 4:12).** The most fundamental belief of the Christian faith is that Jesus of Nazareth is God Himself. This is why the Apostle Paul would say, **"He is the image of the invisible God, the first born over all creation. For in him all things were created: things in heaven and in earth, visible and invisible, weather thrones or powers or rulers or authorities; all things have been created through him and for him. He is before all things, and in him all things hold together. And he is the head of the body, the church; he is the beginning and the first born from among the dead, so that in everything he might have supremacy. For God was pleased to have all his fullness dwell in him, and through him to reconcile to himself all things, whether things on earth or things in heaven, by making peace through the blood, shed on the cross," (Colossians 1:15-22).** See, once mankind was alienated from God and were made enemies in our minds because of evil behavior. But now God has reconciled you and me by Christ's physical body through death to present us holy in God's sight, without blemish and free of accusation... It was this faith in His deity that would later lead Paul, the disciples, and so many early believers to their own martyr's deaths.

Many live in total denial of this coming appointment. One's life's greatest facts is that you are going to die. Lately, it has dawned on me that this body of mine has death in it. I am decaying right before my eyes. Some people opt for plastic surgery, have liposuction, or regularly take handfuls of vitamins and supplements, that's all good for us to do. But none of that can stop the fact that we are marching toward death, our final enemy. **"But, beloved, be not ignorant of this one thing, that one day is with the LORD as a thousand years, and a thousand years as one day. The Lord is not slack concerning his promise, as some men count slackness, but is longsuffering to us-ward,** *not willing that any should perish, but that all should come to repentance.* **But the day of the Lord will come as a thief in the night; in which the heavens shall pass away with great noise,** and the elements shall melt with fervent heat, the earth also and the works that are therein shall be burned up.

Seeing then that all these things shall be dissolved, what manner of persons ought ye to be in all holy conversation and godliness, Looking for and hasting unto the coming of the day of God, wherein the heavens being on fire shall be dissolved, and the elements shall melt with fervent heat?

Nevertheless we, according to his promise, look for new heavens and a new earth, wherein dwelleth righteousness. Wherefore, beloved, seeing that ye look for such things, be diligent that ye may be found of him in peace, without spot, and blameless. And account *that* the long suffering of our Lord *is* salvation; even as our beloved brother Paul also according to the wisdom given unto him hath written unto you; As also in all *his* epistles, speaking in them of these things; in which are some things hard to be understood, which they that are learned and unstable wrest, as *they* do also the other scriptures, unto their own destruction.

Ye therefore, beloved, seeing ye know *these things* before, beware lest ye also, being led away will error of the wicked, fall from your own steadfastness. But grow in grace, and in the knowledge of our Lord and Savior Jesus Christ. To him *be* glory both now and forever. Amen," (2 Peter 3:3-18).

## Salvation

A great provision – at issue here is salvation and whether we will spend eternity with God or apart from Him. God has provided forgiveness and salvation to **whosoever** will come to Him in repentance and faith. It is the free gift of eternal life. It is of little wonder then that the writer uses two qualifying words when speaking of this salvation. First, he describes it as "great." But there is more. He speaks of it as "so" great a salvation.

Our salvation is "so great" because of its ***origin:*** it is great because of the great love that made our salvation possible in the first place. Paul wrote that we who were dead in our sin have been saved **"because of [God's] great love with which He loved us" (Ephesians 2:4).** Our salvation is also great because God's great love not only prompted it, but He also provided it for us. God's great love is always accompanied by His great mercy: **"For as the heavens are high above the earth, so great is His mercy toward those who fear Him," (Psalm 103:11).**

Our salvation is not only great because of its origin but also because of its outcome. Our salvation is accompanied by great blessings of love, joy, peace, and so much more. Our gracious God has made a great provision for us our "so great a salvation."

"How shall we escape if we neglect so great a salvation?" There are three words that describe the response of every person toward the Gospel: *reject, accept, or neglect.*

*Reject-* Some individuals have flat-out *rejected* the Gospel message.

They have consciously and deliberately refused the gift of eternal life. I have personally spoken to many people along life's pathway who have rejected the message of salvation and said no to the claims of Christ.

*Accepted-* Other people have *accepted* the free gift of eternal life offered them through Jesus Christ our Lord. They have heard the Gospel message, believed it, received it by faith, repented of their sins, and trusted in His finished work to save them. Though undeserving, I thank God each morning that I am counted among these.

*Neglected-* Finally, some individuals see themselves in some sort of spiritual no-man's land. They have neither rejected the Gospel, nor have they accepted it. They are among the vast throng who have *neglected* the divine offer of salvation; they have simply put off the decision for the present. They are deceived into thinking there will always be adequate time to name Jesus as their Savior and Lord before they die.

The writer of Hebrews warned that our hearts can be come hardened (Hebrews 3:8). The Apostle Paul added that those who continue to neglect Jesus' invitation to eternal life can become "past feeling" (Ephesians 4:19). The Greek word found here is callus.

Author Hawkins: "A callus on a hand or even a toe can become so hardened over time that if you stick a pin into it you cannot feel any pain. That skin is "past feeling". And this same kind of callus can appear on a human heart that continues to neglect the call of the Gospel. Every time God calls us, and we decide to postpone our decision, the callus on our heart gets a bit thicker. As He continues to call us unto Himself, and we continue to neglect the call, our hearts can become so hardened that, like the callus on a toe or finger, we cannot sense Him. We are "past feeling."

Perhaps there is someone reading these words at this very moment who would never put off paying their bills or running their business or studying for class. Somehow, tragically, some think it is different with the spiritual matters of the soul. Hell is full of people who had good intentions of one day seriously considering and even accepting Jesus' invitation, but they never seemed to get around to making spiritual matters a priority. God offers you and me salvation…And not just salvation, but great salvation…And not just great salvation, but so great a salvation! How shall we escape…if we neglect it?"

## CHAPTER FIFTEEN

## A New Way of Life

The Power of Thoughts – Renewing the Mind & Guarding the Heart

"The heart is deceitful above all things and beyond cure. Who can understand it? I the LORD search the heart and examine the mind, to reward each person according to their conduct, according to what their deeds deserve."(Proverbs 17:9-10)

To live right we have to change our minds. **"Do not conform to the pattern of this world, but be transformed by the renewing of your mind. Then you will be able to test and approve what God's will is—His good, pleasing and perfect will." (Romans 12:2 NIV)**

If we are honest, most of us know and have experienced that in life we undergo all kinds of trails, interruptions, many times unplanned incidents, unexpected suffering including poor choices that affect everyone we love. The truth is, I wasn't always in covenant with God, and I didn't always guard my heart, but now am learning because I don't like places of pain no one does, so we have to guard our heart. **"Keep thy heart with all diligence; for out of it *are* the issues of life." (Proverbs 4:23KJV)**

As Christians, we still need to hear both the Law and the Gospel. We need to hear the law because, we are all, even after we are saved, ***prone to wander in an "I can do it"*** direction. The Law, said Martin Luther, is a divinely sent Hercules to attack and kill the monster of self-righteousness.

And then we are once crushed again by the Law, we need to be reminded that Jesus paid it all. Even in the life of the Christian, the Law continues to drive us back to Christ—to *that* man's Cross, to *that* man's blood, to *that* man's righteousness.

If you are praying for a sick friend, a spouse, a loss in the family or life has been rough…hold on unswervingly to the LORD's promises, and rest in His faithfulness. **"Therefore I tell you, whatever you ask for in prayer believe that you have received it, and it will be yours. And when you stand praying, if you hold anything against anyone, forgive them, so that your Father in heaven may forgive you your sins," (Mark 11:24).** Sometimes l didn't model respect, neither did I always acknowledge my own failures as a parent. Sometimes, we actually convince ourselves that this is a good thing: Good, we think, God doesn't care about my embarrassing actions; He sees my good intentions. It never takes too long, for us to realize that, most of the time, our intentions are even more embarrassing than our actions. We survive other people seeing the things we do. But can you imagine surviving other people seeing what you think? Today, remember that we have a Savior whose work is more profound than just covering our sinful exteriors. He sees, knows, and forgives (on account of His death and resurrection for us) our wicked insiders along with our wicked outsides. Our part is to; **"Start children off on the way they should go, and even when they are old they will not turn from it."(Proverbs 22:6)**

You may feel frustrated with the pace of your progress, but God is never in a hurry. He took eighty years to prepare Moses, including forty in the wilderness. When God makes a mushroom, He does it overnight; when He makes a giant oak, He takes a hundred years. God sets the schedule, not us. When you get discouraged about how far your loved one still has to go, remember He's still working on *you* all these years and be gracious.

Stop and look at how far God has brought you. In the story of reality, God is both the author and star, and we are really just supporting characters. Christ is the hero; we are His sidekicks. The choices we make usually place ourselves in the starring role;

we are always the protagonists in our own imaginations. But this is a kind of bondage. Thank God that, in Christ, He delivers us from it. Choosing our own adventure seems like the way to go, but it inevitably leads to catastrophe. Only trusting in Christ's finished work leads us to rest from our self-interested "analysis paralysis."

Keep in faith and thank God for what He has already done for us in Christ. The battle is the LORD's! Stand on His Word and find rest in Him. **"Now a slave has no permanent place in the family, but a son belongs to it forever. So if the Son sets you free, you will be free indeed," (John 8:35-36)**. God is faithful, He has promised that our prayers will not go unanswered: **"In my alarm I said, 'I am cut off from your sight!' Yet you heard my cry for mercy when I called to you for help," (Psalm 31:22).** Remember all His faithfulness; God will not fail you, not now, not ever. Jesus is also interceding for all the Saints: **"Neither pray I for these alone, but for them also which shall believe on me through their word; That they all may be one; as thou, Father, art in me, and I in thee, that they also may be one in us: that the world may believe that thou hast sent me," (John 17:20-21).** God is able to do infinitely beyond all our highest prayers or thoughts. Nothing is impossible with God! I thank the LORD that when I praise Him and bring my requests to Him in simple faith. I plug into His almighty power…that when I offer a sacrifice of thanksgiving, I open a door for God to rescue me and bless my life, and I prepare the way for Him to rescue and bless other people, near and far. **"He who offers a sacrifice of thanksgiving honors Me…," (Psalm 50:23).** We worship Him and honor Him in our giving, and we are blessed in the process.

We have a way of forgetting yesterday's blessings, especially when we become immersed in today's burdens. When we only have eyes for "now"—discouragement comes easily. The Scriptures urges us: **"Come unto me, all ye that labor and are heavily laden, and I will give you rest. Take my yoke upon you, and learn from me, for I am meek and lowly in heart: and you shall find rest unto your souls. For my yoke is easy and my burden is light." Mathew 11:28-30)**

## What's in Your Hand?

It's easy to focus on what we feel we've lost through the course of life, but God says He will restore all that you have lost. **"Yes, my soul, find rest in God; my hope comes from him. Truly he is my rock and my salvation; he is my fortress, I will not be shaken. My salvation and my honor depend on God; he is my mighty rock, my refuge. Trust in him at all times, you people; pour out your hearts to him, for God is our refuge." (Psalm 62: 5-8)**

Author Joel Osteen writes: "Stop confessing negativity, things like I don't have the talent, education, or the right personality for such a job. As long as you think you are lacking, this will keep you from God's best. God has given all of us something that we enjoy doing, or comes easily, it's not enough to just have faith in God. That's most important, but you should take it one step further, and have faith in what God has given you. You have to believe you are equipped, empowered, and talented, you have the resources and the personality, everything you need to fulfill your destiny. That is faith, without faith it's impossible to please God. The God you serve is just, compassionate, able and willing to meet your needs, so keep praying and believing. Your need moves God's heart, but your *faith* moves Him to action."

Sooner or later you have to step out of the boat and actually do something with what God has given you; He will get you to where you are supposed to be. We grow from strength-to-strength, so, let God show you where to go. Where you are matters. You can't grow bananas in Alaska, but you can grow them in Jamaica. What's the point? Simply this: Sometimes you need to change your location in order to succeed in what God's called you to do. Look at the life of Elijah. The word of the Lord came to him, saying, **"Get away from here and turn eastward, and hide by the Brook Cherith, which flows into the Jordan. And it will be that you shall drink from the brook, and I have commanded the ravens to feed you there."' (1 King 17:2-4 NKJV).**

Ravens normally don't deliver food; they eat it. But when you do what God tells you and go where He sends you, you move from the natural realm to the supernatural one. God not only has a *plan* for your life. He has a *place* for it. Yes, you must have the right strategy, but you must also be in the right *spot*. **"I am the Lord your God, who teaches you what is best for you, who directs you in the way you should go," (Isaiah 48:17 NIV).**

If your heart's desire is to honor God in all things, He will show you the best location to succeed in. Indeed, He will go ahead of you and rearrange circumstances to your advantage. He did it for Abraham. **"By faith Abraham, when called to go to a place he would later receive as his inheritance, obeyed and went, even though he did not know where he was going," (Heb 11:8 NIV).**

The five years that I was unemployed were the toughest and most challenging. But most importantly, that is the time I felt most close to the Lord. For a while I had been trusting the LORD for work. No doors seemed to open, people talked, l lost friends, but through it all l learned to trust in Jesus. I learned to trust in God, and I learned to depend upon His Word. It's not what I did, God knows there's no good thing in our carnal man, and it's what God has already done for me and you in His son Jesus Christ that we can rest. Your past will never defeat God's dreams for you!

Were there many disappointing reports? Yes, there were. A bread winner, paying bills, supporting my daughter and son including supporting my aging parents back in Africa at the time, I pretty much felt on top of my game. But remember the Scriptures, unless the LORD builds the house, the builders labor in vain. Unless the LORD watches over the city, the guards stand watch in vain. If you don't let God to sit in your driver sit, your labor is vain. (See Psalm 127:1).

As I mentioned in earlier chapters and in my first book, *Grace*, as a single parent I hung on my job and worked 16-hour days, almost five out of seven days. My job became an "idol" that I served trustingly. I always worried, *what if l fall sick, who will pay my bills, or feed my family, what about my family back in Africa?* Slowly, I'd pushed prayer out of my life. I depended on my job and couldn't fathom losing it. That too brings in fear, the scriptures teaches that fear hath torment and is not of God. Not being in control can be a scary thing, but once we face our flaws, we find that our errors, our public disgraces have been given to Christ, secure in the knowledge that when God regards us, He sees only His blameless Son, Jesus Christ. God loves us just as we are, but He loves us too much to leave us there!

How often we forget and must be brought again and again into contact with the truth day-by-day. Our righteousness is secured by the perfection of another, and this righteousness has been gifted to us with no expectation of recompense. The way in which we commonly view the world (that we are the center of things, in control, and will get what we deserve) is so profoundly backward that it takes a profound event (a humble deity dying a criminal's death) to recalibrate us.

As the days pass and we forget, as we inevitably will, the ugly truth about the world and about ourselves, let us rest on the truth that the "profound event" of the gospel of Jesus Christ's life, death, and resurrection has happened, and that it alone can recalibrate us, give us hope, and offer true perspective.

## The Pressure's Off

When the burdens are too heavy, and the voices become louder, when your human strength fails, and there is no cure, when a child dies and the hurt is too deep, when all you know to do is useless and all the money in the world becomes irrelevant to your circumstances and the heartache too deep and still the doom won't go away...*there are open arms in Christ Jesus, He is the hope of all glory! He didn't leave us forsaken. He sent a helping hand, the Holy Spirit.* It might take a little while but if you stop focusing on yourself and hearing those other accusatory voices but instead you choose to cry out to the Lord. God will empower you through His Spirit and will give you the ability to overcome your circumstances, instead of your circumstances overcoming you.

There were days that were very difficult, and those days will surely come. When I wanted nothing else in the world but to hug my mother, to be there for her and with her, instead of thousands of miles away, days when she turned eighty and needed a helping hand, days when she was lonely, and I couldn't be there. When I wished I could take her for a walk, or times when I just really wanted to be able to comfort her and be with her in person when she had a third stroke. To be able to pray with her, hold her hand, during her time of need especially when dad went to be with the Lord...but I couldn't, because of my circumstances. That's when you have to stand aside and see the salvation of the Lord, for the battle is not yours but the LORD's! **"The arrogant dig pits to trap me, contrary to your law. All your commands are trustworthy; help me, for I am being persecuted without cause. They almost wiped me from the earth, but I have not forsaken your precepts. In your unfailing love preserve my life, that I may obey the statutes of your mouth. Your word, LORD, is eternal; it stands firm in the heavens. Your faithfulness continues through all generations; you established the earth, and it endures. Your laws endure to this day, for all things serve you. If your law had not been my delight, I would have perished in my affliction. I will never forget your precepts, for by them you have preserved my life. Save me, for I am yours; I have sought out your precepts. The wicked are waiting to destroy me, but I will ponder your statutes. To all perfection I see a limit, but your commands are boundless." (Psalm 119:85-96)**

We can be so blinded as who gives us life to live, the ability to be able to secure a job and reach out to our loved ones...there comes a day when you have to acknowledge that all along, it's only by God's grace that any good thing happens through us. But the spirit of pride will blind you to take God's glory. God wants us to depend on Him and to acknowledge Him as our only source, not other people. Yes, God uses people, but we are not to expect people even close relatives to meet our needs. God expects us to rely on Him alone, and He chooses how to meet our needs in different ways at different times of our lives, as we continue to walk in obedience to His Word and under the guidance of the Holy Spirit. This is a time when we can grow spiritually when we choose to yield to the leading of the Holy Spirit and depend wholly on God as our only source of supply.

The Gospel liberates us to be okay with not being okay. We know we are not okay-though we try very hard to convince ourselves and other people that we're basically fine. The Gospel effectively tells us. "Relax. It is finished. The pressure's off." Because of the Gospel, we have nothing to prove or protect. We can stop pretending. We can take off our masks and be real. The Gospel frees us from trying to impress people, appease people, or measure up for people. The Gospel frees us from the burden of trying to control what other people think about us. It frees us from the miserable, unquenchable pursuit to make something of ourselves by using others.

The Gospel frees us from what one writer called, "the law of capability"- the law, he said, "that judges us wanting if we are not capable, if we cannot handle it all, if we are not competent to balance our diverse commitments without a slip." The Gospel grants us the strength to admit we're weak and needy and restless-knowing that Christ's finished work has proven to be all the strength, fulfillment, and appease we could ever want, and more. Because Jesus is our strength, our weaknesses don't threaten our sense of worth and value. Now we're free to admit our wrongs and weaknesses without feeling as if our flesh is being ripped off our bones.

When we understand that our significance, security, and identity are all anchored in Christ, we don't have to win-we're free to lose. And nothing in this broken world can beat a person who isn't afraid to lose. We'll be free to say crazy, risky, counterintuitive stuff such as, "To live is Christ and to die is gain!"

Real, pure, unadulterated freedom happens when the resources of the Gospel crush any sense of need to secure for ourselves anything beyond what Christ has already secured for us!

**"The LORD is my refuge,' and you make the most high your dwelling, no harm will overtake you, no disaster will come near your tent. For he will command His angels concerning you to guard you in all your ways; they will lift you up in their**

**hands, so that you will not strike your foot against a stone. You will tread on the lion and the cobra; you will trample the great lion and the serpent. Because he loves me, "says the LORD, "I will rescue him; I will protect him, for he acknowledges my name. He will call on me, and I will answer him; I will be with him in *trouble*, I will deliver him and honor him. With long life I will satisfy him and show him my salvation." (Psalm 91:9-16)**

# CHAPTER SIXTEEN

## Christ's Hands And Feet

God uses people; we are His hands and eyes. God loves other people through us, through our loving others, through our giving, even a simple smile, a kind word and so forth goes a long way, and in most cases touches people in ways we will sometimes never know or realize. However, our attitudes have to be in the right place. We love because God first loved us, and we therefore must give the Lord all glory for all that He does through us for others for we are members of the same body in Christ Jesus. Not taking pride as if we accomplished anything on our own, for what do we have that we did not receive...otherwise if we do it out of show, and lack comes, our egos are crushed and we are embarrassed because we do not want to admit failure, or lack to others looking on because the pride of life wants to claim glory that's due God! **"But may it never be that I should boast, except in the cross of our Lord Jesus Christ..." (Galatians 6:14)**

I am reminded constantly that I am a vessel God chooses to use even with my many imperfections, to His glory, but apart from me He has way too many ways and means and others He will use to accomplish His purposes if we're not available. God is not limited by you or me. God has always been our source of supply; He is now and always will be! He expects His children to know through his Word that all good things come from Him. It is very important to acknowledge His providence. I also praise Him for continued faithfulness all through my life, and especially, over the past few years when all seemed to be lost! Our God is awesome! When we are suffering, our need for God is greater than ever. The more we choose to draw near to Him, affirming our trust in Him, the more we can find hope in *His unfailing Love.* You can even learn to be joyful in hope while waiting in His Presence - where joy abounds. Persevere in trusting Him, and God will eventually *lift you up.* Meanwhile, *cast all your anxiety on Him,* knowing that *He cares for you.* He wants to do the same for all His children, take refuge in Him, God will never let you down! **"Surely he will save you from the fowler's snare and from the deadly pestilence. He will cover you with his feathers, his faithfulness will be your shield and rampart..." (Psalm 91:3-4).** The just shall live by faith, and without faith it's impossible to please God.

Even though all I really wanted was to provide for my mother at all times, a responsibility I whole-heartedly prided in and took for granted. The attitude was wrong, many things were wrong, and God was no longer in His rightful place in my life. Maybe if I hadn't been stripped of everything, I would have headed a different route. But I thank God for the role all these difficult things have played in my life. Not all things are God sent but they are all God used!

We can be so blinded and full of ourselves, but thank God, the Lord does not leave us there. If we open our mouth with words of faith according to His will for us, God will fulfill it. He does not treat us as our sins deserve.

It is God who has provided for, watched over and kept my mother despite my circumstances. Yes, He might have used me occasionally, but God is not limited by my joblessness or lack thereof, he has used my daughter and my other sisters, God has provided for her and for me in numerous and unforeseen ways. He's faithful and He does not change; God is the same, yesterday, today and forever. In the natural, life can be brutal, but thank God the battle is not ours but the LORD's, and He says He will not allow us to go through what we cannot handle. **"So, if you think you are standing firm, be careful that you don't fall! No temptation has overtaken you except what is common to mankind. And God is faithful; he will not let you to be tempted beyond what you can bear. But when you are tempted, he will also provide a way out so that you can endure it,"(1 Cor.10:12-13).** The Scripture teaches; **"...the just shall live by faith," (Habakkuk 2:4).** And in addition to faith, we must add prayer, the Word of God, and most importantly is, our relationship with our Helper, the Comforter, and the Holy Spirit, who will teach us in all truths. **"…you yourselves know what happened throughout all Judea, beginning from Galilee after the baptism that John proclaimed: how God anointed Jesus of Nazareth with the Holy Spirit and with Power. He went about doing good and healing all who were oppressed by the devil, for God was with Him. (Acts 10:37-38)**

Have you ever had an encounter that you could describe like Paul does, as full of power and the Holy Spirit? My prayer for all of us is that we would have nothing short of a transformative encounter with the Spirit of God, and that this encounter with God would not only edify and strengthen us with the energy to carry out our God-given callings and tasks in and for this world Jesus loves. **"May the God of hope fill you with all joy and peace in believing, so that by the power of the Holy Spirit you may abound in hope."(Romans 15:13 ESV)**

### The Life of God in Us

Who is your anchor? Your husband, wife, children, job, house, or investments? Who you really are is not the job you have, the car you drive or the house you live in! You are a spirit being having a human experience. We read in the Scriptures in the book of Genesis that: **"And the LORD God formed a man from the dust of the ground and breathed into his nostrils the breath of life, and the man became a living thing," (Gen.2:7).** In other words, there is a relationship between breath, wind, divine inspiration, intellect and soul. The soul (nephesh) of a man is connected to the breath of God—housed in flesh and formed from dust. This tells us that as soon as you become a living soul, your spirit and mind are connected to God. But because we have power to choose…our will…we find ourselves engaged in daily battle of deciding between the carnal mind, and a spiritual mind.

"Carnal" means having the nature of the flesh, sensual, or controlled by animal appetites. Our "carnal mind" is therefore controlled by the flesh – which will ultimately die. **"By the sweat of your brow you will eat your food until you return to the**

**ground, since from it you were taken; for dust you are and to dust you shall return." (Genesis 3:19)**

"Spiritual" means made of wind or breath that is spacious…"air in motion." The Holy Spirit is as a current of air from God…the breath of Our Lord! "Spirit Mind" is connected to and controlled by the Spirit of Christ…it is the eternal spirit of God that will never die. Because we have the power to choose, we find ourselves engaged in a daily battle of deciding between life and death. **"For to be carnally minded is death, but to be spiritually minded is life and peace," (Romans 8:6).**

In the book of Romans, we are instructed not to conform to the pattern of this world but be transformed by the renewing of your mind. Then you will be able to test and approve what God's will is—his good, pleasing and perfect will." (See Romans 12:2) To be **"transformed"** means **your mind must undergo a renovatio**n…which means **to restore to an earlier condition,** as by repairing or remodeling…*Christ came along to give us our mind back!*

Once a person is filled with the Spirit, the Holy Ghost begins each day to bring to his or her remembrance everything that God spoke over them when they were a "Word" out of His mouth – before they were formed with a body. **"For you created my inmost being; you knit me together in my mother's womb. I praise you because I am fearfully and wonderfully made; your works are wonderful, I know that full well. My frame was not hidden from you when I was made in the secret place, when I was woven together in the depth of the earth. Your eyes saw my unformed body; all the days ordained for me were written in your book before one of them came to be." (Psalms 139:13-16)** By and through the Spirit, we have begun to "remember", to "recall" His voice—and, recollect our predestined inheritance! You have to renew your mind back to the start…where you began in the loins of the Father- and then start walking, talking, and living the way He initially designed and purposed. It's about rediscovering your real, true, God-given identity, in the image of Christ, which means you have to get back to your "essential character"…your real identity, created in the Image of God.

Who we really are is NOT based upon race, place, face or background! If you don't know who you are in Christ, you will never know what you have…and can be, and attain, in and through Christ. That's why it is written: **"For in Him we live, we move and have our being."(Acts 17:28)**

# CHAPTER SEVENTEEN

## Molds, Our False Ideas & Mirrors

"These false ideas create "MOLDS" in your mind – Our learned thoughts, patterns and paradigms---create our mindset, formed by various inputs into our lives; religion, learned behavior, negative words, failure, hurt from previous experiences and the list goes on – these false ideas create "MOLDS" and are resistant to change. These molds and mindsets create distorted self-perceptions …You can actually be living and experiencing life having an identity crisis—"a state of confusion regarding a person's nature or direction. Your sense of who you are—your identity—can be skewed if you have others as your mirror to judge your self-worth. But this is how our identity is formed as very young children. If someone made us to feel worthwhile and accepted us, we believed we were okay. But then, if someone treated us badly, or rejected us, then we perceived ourselves as "bad" – and believed that this badness was intrinsic part of who we were (and therefore, in some way, we were unworthy).

Most people don't realize they live with these molds…which limit and restrict your view of yourself…your identity. (They also limit and restrict your view of the world!) To discover your true identity, you must BREAK THE MOLD – and find the "right mirror" to view yourself in – The Word of God. **"For the word of the LORD is right and true; he is faithful in all he does." (Psalm 33:4)**

(Proverbs 4:23) You must be the gatekeeper of your heart (soul/mind) - and to monitor what comes in and what comes out of our "spirit" being. If you know that your life isn't going in the direction you believe God intended for you, you must make the determined decision to change the way you are thinking – to refocus the direction of your thoughts.

**"We know that the law is spiritual; but I am unspiritual, sold as a slave to sin. I do not understand what I do. For what I want to do I do not do, but what I hate to do I do. And if I do what I do not want to do, I agree that the law is good. As it is, it is no longer I myself who do it, but it is sin living in me. For I know that good itself does not dwell in me, that is, in my sinful nature. For I have the desire to do what is good, but I cannot carry it out. For I do not do the good I want to do, but the evil I do not want to do- this I keep on doing," (Romans 7:14-19).** The vital truth Paul wants all of us to accept is; *What controls our Mind Controls Our life!*

The mind is the seat of spiritual and carnal conflict. It is within your mind that your victory…or defeat…begins and ends. It is your mind that determines whether the outcome of your actions will culminate in success…or failure. It is absolutely critical to understand that the flesh…our flesh…and the spirit…our spirit…are in conflict…whether we want to be or not. As long as we're in this Earth, our flesh will forever house sin that will never be fully vanquished…because sin is part of our flesh nature. Even believers are not safe from this "sin that lives within." But there's a major soul-comforting difference between our guilt and that of unbelievers. The redeemed person has been justified of all sins and has been washed through regeneration. **"…he has saved us, not because of righteous things we had done, but because of his mercy. He saved us through the washing or rebirth and renewal by the Holy Spirit, whom he poured out on us generously through Jesus Christ our Savior, so that, having been justified by his grace, we might become heirs having the hope of eternal life," (Titus 3:5-7).** What amazing grace and mercy!

We are in the midst of an on-going and perpetual war – made even more dangerous because it is going on inside our minds, bodies and souls, while we are going on about our lives, daily! As awful as it is to accept, it is a very real truth that satanic forces try to control your thinking through your flesh…which is connected to the five senses. The flesh literally has its own mind – and it is a sinful one.

The mind of our sinful flesh purposely sets its desires against the mind of the spirit! This is why it is vital to understand: your mind is a place of constant warring, spirit against flesh – your mind is literally a battlefield. Paul goes on to share in **verses 20-25**. He attempts to clarify the opposing forces that operate within him (us) that causes him to be a *"wretched man."* He, like us, is aware of an ongoing struggle against the goodness in our *"inner being"* that finds *"delight in God's law"* – verses the other law – *"the law of sin at work within my members."* Ultimately, he realizes that it is within his MIND that God's law must remain pre-eminent…even as the sin of the law of the flesh – what he calls *"this body of death"* –tries to assert its evil intentions in order to gain influence over his (our) mind.

The flesh is so difficult to control; it's the negatives in our lives that God will use to get us to crawl under His rescue. And he'll allow the process to go on a little longer until our spirit gets power over our stubborn flesh. The effect of the Gospel on sinners is not in the impressiveness of Christians or their eloquent arguments, but in the Gospel itself. Paul writes in 1 Corinthians 2:1-5:

**"And I, when I came to you, brothers, did not come proclaiming to you the testimony of God with lofty speech or wisdom. For I decided to know nothing among you except Jesus Christ and him crucified. And I was with you in weakness and in fear and much trembling, and my speech and my message were not in plausible words of wisdom, but in demonstration of the Spirit and of power, so that your faith might not rest in the wisdom of men but in the power of God."(ESV)**

And this is certainly reflective of the Gospel itself; ***which tells us that God the Most High has come to the lowest of men- you and me- in order to redeem us***. Whether battling our thought life or other defeating habits, our human determination will not cut it! It's the attitude of the heart that makes the critical difference between the LORD's acceptance, or rejection of our

"RIGHTEOUSNESS". We are only the righteousness of God when we are in *Christ Jesus*. **"I am the vine; you are the branches. If you remain in me and I in you, you will bear much fruit; apart from me you can do nothing,"(John 15:5).** Our own strength can avail nothing. Faith in Christ alone will produce a mysterious change in our outward actions.

## Legalism

Legalism could be described as trying to earn God's favor by performing a set of behaviors and abstaining from others. Legalism is when man assigns weight to certain actions and gives his own self-credit for performing or not performing said actions, resulting in a system of self-righteousness inside the heart and creating a separation from God because now the person is following after their own system of self-righteousness. In short legalism is man's own righteous acts apart from God…this is pure evil. **"But when he saw many of the Pharisees and Sadducees coming to where he was baptizing, he said to them: "You brood of Vipers! Who warned you to flee from the coming wrath?" (Mathew 3:7)** Jesus, who is true holiness, refers to the Pharisees as "generation of vipers!" Their doctrine, legalism, was labeled by Him as pure evil and demonic. Jesus asks them how they would escape the fires of hell! Anything we try to do to score points with God that is not Christ centered, is a dead work! In the following Scripture, Jesus uses such strong language against the Pharisees, the Sadducees and the teachers of the law: "You snakes! You brood of vipers! How will you escape being damned to hell?" **(Mathew 23:33)**

Normally when we think of people in need of God's rescuing grace, we think of the unrighteous and the immoral. But what's fascinating is that throughout the Bible, it's the immoral person who understands the Gospel before the moral person. It's the prostitute who understands grace; it's the Pharisee who doesn't.

What we see in **(Luke 7:36-50)** is that God's grace wrecks and then rescues, not only the promiscuous but the pious. The

Pharisee in this story can't understand what Jesus is doing by allowing this woman to touch him, because he assumes that God is for the clean and competent. But Jesus here shows him that God is for the unclean and incompetent and *when measured against God's perfect holiness, we're all unclean and incompetent.* Jesus shows him that the Gospel isn't for the well behaved, but the dead." Jesus came not to affect a moral reformation but a moral resurrection. Everywhere else in the world, loveliness precedes love. Only in the Gospel does love precede loveliness.

*As Gerhard Forde puts it, "Christianity is not the move from vice to virtue, but rather the move is from virtue to grace."*

Wrecking every religious virtue category, the Pharisee had, Jesus tells him that he has a lot to learn from the prostitute, not the other way around.

The prostitute walks into a party of religious people and falls at the feet of Jesus without any care as to what others are thinking and saying. She's at the end of herself. More than wanting to avoid an uncomfortable situation, she wanted to be clean-she, and needed to be forgiven. She was acutely aware of her guilt and shame. She knew she needed help. She understood at a profound level that God's grace didn't demand that she get clean before she came to Jesus. Rather, her only hope for getting clean was to come to Jesus. ***Jesus is calling you to come as you are!***

God wants us to be truthful, and to examine our own hearts, to be willing to change and go in the direction we know Jesus Christ would have us go in. A heart of obedience and alliance to God is what His heart seeks after. He wants a relationship with you. God cares about every little thing in your life. **"You do not delight in sacrifice, or I would bring it; you do not take pleasure in burnt offerings. My sacrifice, O God, is a broken spirit; you, God, will not despise."(Psalm 51:16-17)**

# CHAPTER EIGHTEEN

## Empowered To Succeed

We simply cannot fulfill the mission God has called us to without walking in the **power** of the **Holy Spirit.** We neglect the Holy Spirit to our own detriment. Without actively walking in power of the Holy Spirit we will not be able to walk to fulfill our God ordained mission. We need our *"the Helper"*, as He is referred to by Jesus in John 14, most of us are barely making it, if we are even making it at all. Lots of us are bluffing our way through the Christian life, yet we don't need to because there is a better way and that better way is, life lived in the fullness of the Spirit.

Therefore, pray to God to remove from your eyes every scale that is preventing you from seeing and walking in the truth of God's Word. Ephesians also says**: "Do not grieve the Holy Spirit of God, with whom you were sealed for the day of redemption." (Ephesians 4:30)**

In this book, *Flame of Love: A Theology of the Holy Spirit,* Clark Pinnock suggests that we wrongly tend to think of the Spirit as antithetical to matter.

Author Beth Moore referring to this quote says, I think what Pinnock says is helpful and also true:

*"When Jesus says that God is spirit, it is not that God is ghostly but that God is the power of creation, the incalculable energy that can give life to the dead and call things that do not exist into being (Romans 4:17)...It is easy for us to be misled about the meaning of the Spirit, since in Western languages and philosophies we think of it standing in antithesis to matter. So when we hear that God is Spirit, we think in terms of Platonic ideas and in corporeality. But spirit in the Bible has to do less*

*Beauty for Ashes*

*with immateriality than with power and life—the invisible, mysterious power of a gale-force wind that we can-not begin to track.* **"The wind blows wherever it pleases. You hear its sound, but you cannot tell where it comes from or where it is going. So it is with everyone born of the Spirit. (John 3:8).** *Spirit is the Bible's way of speaking of what we would call the transcendent power of creation."*

**"But you will receive power when the Holy Spirit has come upon you, and you will be my witnesses in Jerusalem and in all Judea and in Samaria, and to the end of the earth." (Acts: 1:8)** The Holy Spirit is our comforter and guidance. The real truth is when you learn to hear and to yield to the guidance of the Holy Spirit, you will be amazed at what you can do in Christ to God's glory. **"Howbeit, when he, the Spirit of truth, is come, he will guide you in all truth: for he shall not speak of himself; but whatsoever he shall hear, that shall he speak: and he will show you things to come. He shall glorify me: for he shall receive of mine, and shall show *it* unto you." (John 13-14)**

I exult in God's marvelous grace-His favor and blessings which I do not deserve- for He has raised me up with Christ and seated me with Him in the heavenly realm, far above any conceivable command, authority, power, or control. **"The Spirit Himself bears witness with our spirit that we are children of God..." (Romans 8:16)** God has given me and you an exalted status in His Kingdom- in the one realm where being included and honored has any real significance, any lasting value.

In Christ we have been linked to the greatest possible purposes, the highest of all reasons for living: to know and love Him...and to show His love to other people...to glorify Him...and to enjoy His love now and forever. What an honor! If I had continued beating myself up, or looking back at all that had failed or gone wrong...I highly doubt that I would have written my first, second and now my third book in the making? Probably not. It's been by God's grace! I thank the Lord that In Christ I live, I move I have my being. Every good thing I do comes from the Lord and I give Him all the glory!

Maybe you are thinking, well you can afford it, and you are right…in Christ I have everything I need for my calling…in the physical I don't have to have money in my account to write my testimony, to encourage a broken heart, to lift up those who are bowed down…money cannot limit me in what am called to do. I have a part to play and God has a part to fulfill. Do your part by faith and trust God who is faithful to bring your desire to pass to His glory. I have faith that God will honor His part. *Seeking first His kingdom, and all these things shall be added unto us*. You are waiting for God to do something, while He's waiting for *you* to take that step of faith by stepping out of the boat like Peter. Peter walked on the Word of God and walked on water, and so can we. Without stepping out of the boat, without walking on His Word, how will we know if we can indeed walk on the water…how can we see the miraculous happen in our lives?

You keep saying eventually, and I hope and pray that your *"eventually"* for you is *TODAY*, as you read these lines…***Eventually his own will hear his voice, and something within them will awaken. And when it does, they will begin to sing again.*** Where there is genuine conversion, there is eternal salvation. Our task is to trust God's ability to call His children home. We join God as he walks among His wayward and wounded children, singing, serving, loving, giving, sharing the Good News…being His hands, legs, eyes and all we can be to give all glory to His name. For me it's writing and writing and writing about the Good News, the Gospel and being his legs, hands and eyes. When God lets His light to shine into every remote corner of our mind, it brings revelation, clarity and understanding to us concerning our circumstances and His purpose for our lives.

For it is written: "Arise (from depression and prostration in which circumstances have kept you), rise to new life! Shine (be radiant with the glory of the Lord) for your light has come, and the glory of the Lord is risen upon you! (Isaiah 60:1 AMP)

Meditating on the Word of God and whatever is edifying, makes thinking on what God says more possible. More and more, we begin to hold the feelings and thoughts of the Messiah. God has not given us the spirit of fear but of love, power and a sound mind.

Nobody can do for us what the Holy Spirit can do for us. Every person has seeds of greatness planted within by the Creator for a greater purpose to His glory. It's not about you. It's great to be educated in a profession, I studied secretarial duties and worked in that field for ten years. I also took a Certified Nurses' Aide classes and worked in the nursing profession for twelve years, in both fields I acquired some knowledge that has in one way or another enhanced my journey, so I praise Him for "all things" including these, they have contribute to my spiritual growth and my experience with God. God wants His children to have good knowledge and understanding in whatever area, skill or profession we may desire. As long as we acknowledge Him as our source of supply, and the origin of our gifts, and because God is the one who gives us life, breath and everything else...He has to receive all glory and praise. In our strength, we labor but in vain. **"Except the LORD build the house, they labor in vain that build it: except the LORD keep the city, the watchman waketh** *but* **in vain. (Psalm 127:1)**

God is more constant and unchanging than the sun and moon and stars. We have to acknowledge Him and give Him glory for all the good and the bad He allows in our lives. God breathed into man - His spirit is in us, breathing is living. Christ indwelling a believer is profound life! God is able to pull you together, and put you together, will you trust Him today?

Whatever your case maybe, we serve a God of impossibilities that has promised to shield and to protect us from harm and to bring light and warmth into our lives as we trust Him. So, take the limits off of God. Don't think of all the reasons to do nothing.

If you seek Him with a reverent heart, if you choose to trust Him and go His way instead of your own, more and more He will make you see and experience His great goodness. God has demonstrated His undying love for man by the way of the Cross through His only begotten Son Jesus Christ. God wants you to come as you are, when we say that, **"God catches the wise in**

**their craftiness,"** the way He does it is by continuously raising the bar of requirement until no amount of craftiness can get over it or around it. We will wreck ourselves on the wall of *"be perfect even, as your heavenly father is perfect."* We make a big mistake when we conclude that the Law is the answer to bad behavior. In fact, law alone stirs up more of such behavior. People get worse, not better, when you lay down the law. To be sure, the Spirit does use both God's Law and God's gospel in our sanctification. But the Law and the gospel do very different things. The Law reveals sin, but it is powerless to remove it. It points to righteousness but can't produce it. It shows us what godliness is but cannot make us godly. *As Martin Luther said, "Sin is not canceled by lawful living, for no person is able to live up to the law. Nothing can take away sin except the grace of God."* The Law apart from the Gospel can only crush; it cannot cure.

I have learned from the Scripture, when God calls us, He equips us. **"For those God foreknew he also predestined to be conformed to the image of his Son, that he might be the firstborn among many brothers and sisters. And those he predestined, he also called; those he called, he also justified; those he justified, he also glorified," (Romans 8:29-30).** As great and necessary as it may be to be talented, or to be born in a certain family background, attend a privileged school and so forth, none of these things stop the Spirit of God from empowering you in your calling, as you delight in Him, and seek first the Kingdom of God and His righteousness, His promises follow you. **"But seek first the kingdom of God and his righteousness, and all these things will be given to you as well," (Mathew 6:33).** Your destiny is God ordained and He has all intentions of you fulfilling it *by all means necessary*. Remember, only you can forfeit your own destiny, no one or nothing has the power to, only your hardened heart toward the LORD.

## Choose to forgive and forget

When Adam and Eve disobeyed God, mankind was condemned and therefore fell from their original state of righteousness and holiness (See Romans 5:12-21). But it's important to remember that we are being restored back to the image of God. Another role of the Holy Spirit is to transform our mind and thoughts to be more like Jesus. What makes a difference is God's anointing on your life. The Holy Spirit will guide you and steer you in the right direction as you seek God's face and purpose for your life.

I can't stress enough the power of forgiveness; forgiveness overcomes bitterness and we gain freedom by releasing others from their sins. Forgiveness is for you not them! Put down the baggage and remember the grace of the Almighty God toward you. Receive His forgiveness and let it flow through you to others.

Release others from their sins towards you. You will be amazed at how much peace you experience. Submit to God and His ways of doing things, every good and perfect gift is from Him! Disown sinful influences that come from associations, take responsibility of your own actions to gain full freedom. And love your enemies; love is a choice. If we follow our emotions, we will find it difficult even sometimes impossible to forgive those that have hurt us. That's why we have to overcome the flesh by practicing what the Word says we should do. (See **Mathew 5:43-47**)

When all your life meaning, your significance, your security, your protection, your safety, are all riding on you, it actually feels like slavery. This is a burden we were never meant to bear, and yet after the fall, self- reliance became our default mode of operation. You might even call it our inheritance. In our exile from Eden, we naturally tend to lean toward self-reliance. Fortunately, God does not leave us there. The Gospel is for the defeated not the dominant. In view of God's holiness, we are all losers: **"For all have sinned and fall short of the glory of God, and all are justified freely by his grace through the redemption that came by Christ Jesus."(Romans 3:23-24)**

The Authors Ruth and Warren Myers write: "When you are really saved the devil and his schemes cannot bring you to a place of defeat, because as a believer, you are informed that the Christian life is not a rigorous self-improvement course or a do-it-yourself kit…that it is not a call to prove yourself or improve yourself by overcoming your own shortcomings and failures, in your own way, by yourself with your own resources. But instead understanding that God is at work in your situation to break old patterns of thought and action, to create within you both the desire and the power to do His gracious will…and to make you a joy to Him in new ways, and produce in you the fruits of the Spirit, to enable you to give thanks for all things."

Where there is no assurance of salvation, there is no peace. No peace means no joy. No joy results in fear-based lives. Is this the life God creates? No. Grace creates a confident soul who declares, **"I know whom I have believed, and am convinced that he is able to guard what I have entrusted to him for that day," (2 Tim. 1:12 NIV).** You have to trust on Gods' hold on you more than your hold on Him. His faithfulness does not depend on ours.

Words are a channel through which spiritual power of blessing may be transmitted. Your future is framed by what you say, not what you see. (See **1 John 1: 5-10 & 2:1-2**) The Gospel is for those who have realized that they can't carry the weight of the world on their shoulders. Only when God drives us to the end of ourselves do we begin to see life in the Gospel.

Blessings (and curses) belong to the invisible, spiritual realm. Your success in life depends on being able to apprehend and relate to that which is invisible and spiritual. You must use your words as containers of blessing to others and yourself if you want to walk in blessing. The Bible says that He, **"…makes me lie down in green pastures; he leads me beside still waters." (Ps.23:2)** This verse is a picture of rest, peace, and beauty.

For some of us, the freedom we long for is well in sight, but far out of reach. You can see the promised place, but you just can't get there. You can see the peace, rest and beauty He has for you, but you just don't have it yet. Generational blessing is part of the freedom that the death and resurrection of Jesus Christ gives you the legal right to possess. God wants you to overcome adversity and break free. He has opened the door for freedom for anyone who will believe Him. The world needs you to be who you are in Him!

In my first book, ***GRACE*:** I share how my mother was completely healed, in spite of the doctors' reports that, she was on her deathbed, with only three months to live. It was choosing to stand and believe on God's Word, the finished works that Christ accomplished on the Cross that brought my mother back to health reversing the doctors' reports. There's Power in the Word of God, but it's the authority we exercise that enables a believer to experience the abundant life Christ died for us to have. We made a conscious choice to choose and believe in what God's written word says. **"Your word, LORD, is eternal; it stands firm in the heavens. Your faithfulness continues through all generations; you establish the earth and it endures. Your laws endure to this day, for all things serve you. If your law had not been my delight, I would have perished in my affliction. I will never forget your precepts, for by them you have preserved my life. Save me for I am yours; I have sought out your precepts. The wicked are waiting to destroy me, but I will ponder your statutes. To all perfection I see a limit, but your commands are boundless."(Psalm 119:89-96)**

True faith is when you believe the Word of God in spite of natural evidence to the contrary, God brings dead things to life to His glory. It is believing you're healed even when you still feel sick. It comes from your spirit by the agency of God's WORD and says, "I know I don't feel healed. I know I don't sound healed. I know I don't look healed, that's a **FACT** but what does the **TRUTH** in your Bible say? Believe you are healed because The WORD says so, choose to believe God's Word over your circumstances and overcome by the blood of the Lamb of God, Jesus Christ. The Word of the LORD is right and true! **"For the word of the LORD is right and true; he is faithful in all he does."(Ps.33:4**.) When your mind doubts and says, "I can't believe that!" Your spirit should answer, "I know it. You're not equipped to believe it, but I am. So, I'm taking ascendancy over you. You'll see the evidence of the healing in a while, but until then, I'm ordering you to keep your unbelieving mouth shut. From this point on, I'm in charge and I'm going to speak only words of faith."

Sooner than we expected my mother's improvement became apparent…while she had at first been unable to recognize me, eat or even to talk, she now could call my name, and then she started eating and learning to walk…God's Word was taking effect. We chose not to believe what we saw before our very eyes but instead believed the report of the Lord! This is only one of numerous testimonies of God's miraculous healing in my family!

My sister Judith's daughter Naomi was miraculously rescued and flown to a hospital, where she underwent an emergency operation that saved her life, without that immediate operation, Naomi would have lost her life. That morning before the incident Naomi had read a SCRIPTURE and stood on it the whole day. As Naomi was fainting behind the wheel, a driver who happened to be behind her noticed something was wrong with the driver in front of her and acted by contacting the police. Naomi had had an attack, this happened at night. Anything could have gone wrong. He in His word says: I AM IMMANUEL---GOD WITH YOU---AND I am enough! "God with us." **(Matthew 1:21-23). "Surely he took up our pain and bore our suffering, yet we considered him punished by God, stricken by him, and afflicted. But he was pierced for our transgressions, he was crushed for our iniquities; the punishment that brought peace was on him, and by his wounds we are healed."**(Isaiah 53: 4-5)

We watched Gods' Hand of healing work in my mother's life, mightily, as He restored her back to health. God wants to heal you. He is still JEHOVAH RAPHA – The Lord Who Heals! Glory to the name of Jesus. In spite of what many may see before their eyes as your deserving afflictions and judge you in times of adversity, don't take it as a personal attack, God has allowed these weaknesses, your infirmities, inadequacies (physical, mental, emotional, relational)…all these, that they may contribute to His high purposes for you. Thank God for how He allows them to prod you to trust in Him and not in yourself.

Yes, the arm of flesh will fail you over and over again, turning away from your trials and lack, but what fuels our inner motivations is taking to heart the outpouring of God's love to us. God has spoken and promised to show Himself strong. We must be like little children relying on our heavenly Father's mighty arm. Like Paul, we say that we have no confidence in the flesh but rejoice in Jesus Christ! **(Philippians 3:2-3)**

God must quicken us, enabling us to change our motivation, and to see that all through life in all things He continues to be our sole supply. However, God uses people and those He chooses to use are to be respected and appreciated, but our confidence must remain in God's faithfulness even when those He has used in the past turn their back. Take no offense, maybe God intended to use them for a season. God is faithful; He will make a way for you in the wilderness. It is our part to see our weakness, in earnest desire and longing, convinced of the fact that we cannot help ourselves; we must trust God for divine enablement. No one can rest until resting in Him. Praise, worship and thanksgiving must become part of our daily walk.

Live with expectancy and hope in God's faithfulness to your desires. Darkness may endure for a night, but joy comes in the morning. In your weakness, God's strength is made perfect. **(2 Cor.12:10)** As we live a life of praise no matter what is going on, we'll discover anew, or our rather understanding, of His deep and abiding compassion for us…the strength of His Word to meet our deepest longings and needs. And above all we'll experience the boundless joy of giving God the praise that is His due.

Speaking the WORD is an essential part of "The Buildup" because what we say is what comes to pass. Our words shape our future. What we're saying today is what we'll have tomorrow. Like it or not, we can't get around it. We live in a word-based, word-created, word-directed environment. **"Death and life are in the power of the tongue: and they that love it shall eat the fruit thereof" (Proverbs 18:21).** Or as Jesus put it in Mark 11:23: **"Whosoever shall say to this mountain, 'Be thou removed and be thou cast into the sea;' and shall not doubt in his heart, but shall believe that those things which he saith shall come to pass; he shall have whatsoever he saith." (Mark: 11:23)**

Although we can't escape the fact that our lives are governed by words, we can choose the words under which we live. We can choose words of faith. We can choose words of blessing. If we do, then BLESSING is what we'll have.

How so quickly we are used to instantly forgetting yesterday's victories and the Lord's faithfulness. But God never forgets His children. **"Behold, I stand at the door, and knock: if any man hear my voice, and open the door, I will come in to him, and will sup with him, and he with me." (Rev.3:20)** I look back and see and remember God's faithfulness. Our answer is found in the person of Jesus. Jesus got word that a good friend was dying. Though He was a good way's away, Jesus told His disciples that the illness "is not to death' and that it was actually for God's glory. He waited with his friends before he even began the journey to see His friend. When he got there, not only was Lazarus dead, but he'd been dead for four days.

Lazarus's resurrection was not just another healing. John's gospel systematically escalates Jesus' interactions with humankind. First, He baptized and preached, then He healed the sick, then He raised the dead. But we don't understand. We're like Martha, who could be paraphrased as having said, **"Lord, if you'd gotten here sooner, my brother wouldn't have died."** We want a Jesus who heals the sick because we don't trust Him to raise the dead. Mary and Martha thought that as long as they could get Jesus involved before things got too out of hand, everything would be okay.

Jesus is out to prove one thing: even death is "not to death." Not to Jesus. Jesus has something serious in mind. When Martha came to Jesus, He said, **"I am the resurrection and the life. The one who believes in me will live, even though they die; and whoever lives by believing in me will never die," (v25)**. If we're honest with ourselves, Paul's description of us in Romans 3 is dead on: ruin and misery mark our ways. We're more than sick - we're falling apart. Actually, it's even more than that. We're dead. Jesus Christ is a God who does something so much better than heal the sick. He raises the dead to new life.

## Giving Grace

Grace exceeds the Law, when we center our hearts and life on Jesus and His forgiveness, we will exceed even what the Law demands of us. The Law says, "Thou shalt not covet," but it cannot command you to be generous. Only grace makes you generous. The Law says, "Thou shall not commit murder," but it cannot put love and forgiveness in your heart for someone who has wronged you. Only the love and forgiveness of Jesus can do that in your heart and transform you to love and forgive your enemies and those who have hurt you.

Author Joseph Prince writes: "In every way when you are under grace, not only will you fulfill the commands of the law, you will end up unconsciously and effortlessly exceeding all the demands of the law! That is what God means when He says about the new covenant, *"I will put My laws in their mind and write them on their hearts; and I will be their God, and they shall be my people," (Hebrews 8:10)*. These laws that God writes in our minds and on our hearts are not the Ten Commandments. They exceed the Ten Commandments. They pertain to the royal law of love that flows from the heart of Jesus and fills our minds and hearts." *Truly, "love is the fulfillment of the law" (Romans 13:10)*! He who forgives much, loves much, and he who is loved most, loves best!

Over the years the LORD has seen me through a lot, and I didn't always respond with faith and trust. When we make the same mistake, it leads to slavery. It' not until we can admit that "I am the problem and I am culpable too" that we will ever be able to see the true magic of a Savior who comes to us and sets us free, not because we are innocent, but because we are guilty.

Do you remember in **LUKE 17:5-6**...Jesus told the disciples that they have no faith after they came to Him and asked Him to increase their faith. Isn't that strange, it would seem like requesting for greater faith in the first place is what the disciples ought to be doing? It does seem that way to us, but that's because we suffer under the same delusion as the disciples did. We think we just need a helping hand...

You see, the mistake the disciples made in asking for increased faith was that they were assuming that they had faith in the first place! But Jesus course corrected them pretty quickly, telling them if they even had the tiniest bit of faith, they could do truly miraculous things. Jesus was showing them what the Law shows us; that we're worse off than we think we are. Like the Law, we can assume we are doing fairly well. None of us would admit that we're perfect—we're too smart for that—but we like to think we're not the worst, either. We say, "I'm not perfect, but…" Jesus response shows He didn't come to Earth to improve the pretty good. He didn't even come to build up the not-that-good. Jesus came to create goodness where there was no goodness before. He came to give faith to the faithless and life to the dead. **"It's because of the LORD's great love we are not consumed, for his compassions never fail. They are new every morning; great is His faithfulness."(Lamentations 3:21-23)**

The Bible reminds me of Peter's choice on one stormy night on the Sea of Galilee. Peter was with the other disciples in the boat and Jesus came walking toward them on the water. At first the disciples were frightened and thought they were seeing a ghost. **"But straightaway Jesus spoke unto them, saying, 'Be of good cheer; it is I; be not afraid.' And Peter answered him and said, 'Lord, if it be thou, bid me to come unto thee on the water.' And he said, 'Come,' And when Peter was come down out of the ship, he walked on the water, to go to Jesus, " (Matthew 14:27-29 KJV).** Peter walked on the **Word** Jesus spoke, **"Come."**

Notice Jesus didn't initiate Peter's miracle there. Peter did. He set it in motion by saying, *"Bid me come."* Jesus said, *"Come,"* and the power to walk on water was in that word. Peter chose to connect with that power by faith and got out of the ship. While he was out there doing what no man had ever done before**, he ran into a problem**. *"When he saw the wind boisterous, he was afraid; and beginning to sink, he cried, saying, 'Lord, save me.' And immediately Jesus stretched forth his hand, and caught him, and said unto him, 'O thou of little faith, why did thou doubt?' (Matthew 14:30-31)*

So why was Peter worried about the weather conditions all of a sudden? Because he got his eyes off Jesus and started focusing on natural impossibilities. This place is familiar to me, and frankly to many believers, like Peter we tend to take our focus off Christ, it's essential to remember that this inner strength to do all things comes to us, as we need it, and as we take trusting steps of dependence, moving forward with our eyes on Jesus and not on our circumstances. **"The Lord is my strength and my shield; my heart trusts in Him and I am helped. My heart leaps for joy and I will give thanks to him in song," (Psalm 28:7)**. When we make Jesus our focus instead of our "down times", our mind will remain at rest. Training your mind to make Christ your default "Focus" is not easy. Ask the Holy Spirit to help you in this challenging endeavor, and He will. However, you must be prepared to cooperate with Him. Think about who God is-Creator, Savior, King of kings. Ponder also God's amazing unending love for you. (See **Psalm 8:3-4).** The lesson here is our focus.

This shift in focus from the external to the internal has terrible practical consequences. Turning to the external object of faith, namely Christ and His finished work on our behalf, is the only place to find peace. I guess I write a lot about focus because focusing on my circumstances knocks us down consistently...but it gets better as we immerse in the Word by God's grace and we are rescued by His Spirit. But we have to give Him something to reach for (the Word). Don't get tired of hearing about the power of the Word, try it for yourself, you will be richly rewarded!

"Then Jesus told the disciples, 'This very night you will all fall away on account of me, for it is written: **'I will strike the shepherd, and the sheep of the flock will be scattered.' 'But after I have risen, I will go ahead of you to Galilee.'** Peter replied, **'Even if all fall away on account of you, I never will.' 'Truly I tell you,'** Jesus answered, **'this very night, before the rooster crows, you will disown me three times.'** (Verse 69) 'Now Peter was sitting out on the courtyard, and a servant girl came to him. 'You also were with Jesus of Galilee,' she said. But he denied it before them all. 'I don't know what you are talking about,' he said. Then he went out to another gateway, where another servant girl saw him and said to the people there, 'This fellow was with Jesus of Nazareth.' He denied it again, with an oath: 'I don't know the man.' After a little while, those standing there went to Peter and said, 'Surely you are one of them; your accent gives you away.' Then he began to call down curses, and he swore to them, 'I don't know the man!'

**Immediately a rooster crowed. Then Peter remembered the words Jesus had spoken: 'Before the rooster crows, you will disown me three times.' And he went outside and wept bitterly." (Mathew 26:69-75) But Jesus sending the women with a message to the disciple, made sure he specifically mentioned Peter; "There you will see him, just as he told you."**

I can't count how many times I have disowned our Lord Jesus Christ. I thank Him for He is the Great High Priest...that He is able to save me completely, for He lives forever and prays for me, and for all of us who have come to God through Him. He is the Lord Most High, who rules over the heavens and the Earth, for He made all things by His great power, and He keeps them existing and working by His mighty Word.

**"The LORD makes firm the steps of the one who delights in him; though he may stumble, he will not fall, for the LORD upholds him with his hand,"(Psalm 37:23-24).** Many Christians think that God is perpetually disappointed with them. But because of what Jesus did for us on the Cross, God sees us as friends and children, not as enemies and strangers. God is a good Father, and because we're with Jesus, God's affection for us is unchanging and His approval of us is forever.

God is not interested in what you think you should be or how you should feel. He is not interested in the narrative you construct for yourself or that others construct for you. He may even use suffering to deconstruct that narrative. Rather, He is interested in **you**, the you who suffers, the you who inflicts suffering on others, the you who hides, the you who has bad and good days. And He meets you where you are. Jesus is not the man at the top of the stairs; He is the man at the bottom, the friend of sinners, the Savior of those in need of one. Which is all of us, all of the time.

No one in the Bible is more of a repeat offender than the apostle, Peter. Peter lived with Jesus for three and a half years, witnessed many miracles, and heard His teaching. He had given up everything for the Lord he deeply loved (Matt.19:27), and he loved his Savior more than he had ever loved anyone. And yet his track record was abysmal.

Peter sank when Jesus told him to walk on water; Jesus called him Satan when Peter tried to persuade Jesus that He wouldn't have to die. He fell asleep three times in Gethsemane, despite Jesus asking him to keep watch. Jesus rebuked him for drawing and for using his sword at Christ's arrest. He denied knowing Jesus three times on the night He was tried.

Apart from his being the first to acknowledge that Jesus was the Christ, the Son of God, almost everything he did in the gospels ended in a correction, a rebuke, or just simple failure. Yet, he is designated "the rock". Why? It is no coincidence that Peter was the weakest and the one who recognized who Jesus was. He could recognize the Savior, because he knew how much he needed one. His faith was directly tied to his failure. As one writer accurately puts it, "The great and merciful surprise is that we come to God not by doing it right but by doing it wrong!"

This is proved by one of the most comforting passages in the Bible. When the women find the young man minding the empty tomb on Easter morning, he gives them a message, which names Peter specifically, who must have feared that his relationship with Jesus was over. That disciple who had seemingly done all in his power to ruin his relationship with Christ, and who had, only a few days before, denied even knowing Him at all, was still going to receive a *kept promise*: **"There you will see him, just as he told you."(Mark 16:7)**

Though Peter was an ultimate promise breaker, *as we all are*, Jesus was and ever will be *the ultimate promise keeper*. Even though I have failed Him over and over, and I may many times feel like Peter, yet the LORD never leaves me nor forsakes me. He's always waiting for me to turn to Him, and to trust Him to see me through in all things.

Many well-meaning believers fall into the devil's trap and end up with the wrong belief that God is disappointed or even mad at them or vice versa. Because of this, they begin feeling like hypocrites. I have been here before. This attitude leads to isolating oneself from Christian or Church fellowships, the intimacy they once had with the LORD becomes stagnant. This is not because they are bad people, but because this wrong belief that God is angry with them, they begin premeditated steps to avoid Him. With this mindset the devil wins this battle, for he is a liar and the father of lies.

**"The king's rage is like the roar of a lion; but his favor is like dew on the grass," (Proverbs 19:12).** "The King" in this verse is our Lord Jesus. He is the true King of kings (See Rev.17:14, 19:16). We are not God's objects of wrath. When the King is angry, He is angry at injustice, at the devil, and at what he is doing in your life. God hates sin because of what it's doing in the object of His love. *You and I are God's object of love.*

Author Richard Foster writes: "A spiritual Discipline is an intentionally directed action by which we do what we can do in order to receive from God the ability (or power) to do what we cannot do by direct effort. It is not in us, for example, to love our enemies. If we go out and try very hard to love our enemies, we will fail miserably. Always. This strength, this power to love our enemies—that is, to genuinely and unconditionally love those who curse us and spitefully use us—is simply not within our natural abilities. We cannot do it by ourselves.

But this fact of life does not mean that we do nothing. Far from it! Instead, by an act of the will we choose to take up disciplines of the spiritual life that we can do. These disciplines are all actions of body, mind, and spirit that are within our power to do. Not always and not perfectly, to be sure, but they are things we can do –by choice, by choosing actions of fasting, study, solitude, and so forth.

The Spiritual Disciplines in and of themselves have no merit whatsoever. They possess no righteousness, contain no rectitude. *Their purpose—their only purpose—is to place us before God.* After that, they have come to the end of their tether. But it is enough. Then the grace of God steps in, takes this simple offering of ourselves, and creates out the kind of person who embodies the goodness of God—indeed, a person who can come to the place of truly loving even enemies."

It is vitally important for us to see all this spiritual training in the context of the work and action of God's grace. As the Apostle Paul reminds us, **"It is God who is at work in you, enabling you both to will and to work for his good pleasure," (Phil 2:13).** This, you see, is no "works of righteousness," as it is sometimes called. Even our desiring the with-God life is an action of grace; it is *"prevenient grace,"* say the theologians. We are not just saved by grace; we live by grace. And we pray by grace and fast by grace and study by grace and serve by grace and worship by grace. All the disciplines are permeated by the enabling grace of God.

**"Heaviness in the heart of man maketh it stoop" (Proverbs 12:25)**

The dictionary defines depression as "to be flattened vertically or dispirited." At this point I was entertaining all sorts of lies from the devil but somehow, I just sat there and took it. The word "depression" is not mentioned in Scripture. The closest definition to it is "heaviness." **"Heaviness in the heart of man maketh it stoop." (Proverbs 12:25)**

My deliverance came when I began to focus on what Christ has already done for me at Calvary. In this way, I was believing and confessing to myself that Christ is in His rightful place in every area of my life. When we become constant in prayer, the power of the blood of Jesus will rid our lives of the curse and we'll truly experience the abundant life Christ died for us to live!

If you don't fully grasp what your salvation is, you will pay a penalty for your lack of knowledge, because you are not exercising your authority in Christ. God urges us to get wisdom and knowledge...my people perish because of lack of knowledge.

It doesn't mean that when we die we won't go to Heaven, it just means we do not live the life Christ died for us to live because we do not exercise the authority we have in Christ, and therefore we pay a penalty already paid at the Cross, but thank God that even though: "Bridges are burned, and the transfer is accomplished. Ebbs and flows continue, but they never disqualify. Ups and downs may mark our days, but they will never ban us from His Kingdom. Jesus bottom-lines our lives with grace." – Paula White, *First Things First*

Author Max Lucado writes: "Even more, God stakes His chain on us. **'By his Spirit he has stamped us with his eternal pledge- a sure beginning of what he destined to complete,' (2 Cor. 1:22 MSG**). You've done something similar: engraved your name on a valued ring, etched your identity on a tool or iPad. Cowboys brand cattle with the mark of the ranch. Stamping declares ownership. Through His Spirit, God stamps us. Would-be takers are repelled by the presence of His name. Satan is driven back by the declaration: *Hands off. This child is mine! Eternally, God."*

On-and-off salvation never appears in the Bible. Salvation is not a repeated phenomenon. Scripture contains no example of a person who was saved, then lost, then resaved, then lost again. When your identity is anchored in Christ, you can say, *"Everything I need I already possess in Him"*, this belief during suffering drives you deeper into your source of joy – the LORD Jesus Christ.

**"So I say, walk by the Spirit, and you will not gratify the desires of the flesh. For the flesh desires what is contrary to the Spirit, and the Spirit what is contrary to the flesh. They are in contrary with each other, so that you are not to do whatever you want. But if you are led by the Spirit, you are not under the law." (Galatians 5:16-18 NIV)**

Suffering in other words, shows us where we are locating our identity. Our response to suffering reveals what we're building our lives on and what we're depending on to make life worth living. This means that suffering itself does not rob you of joy, idolatry does. If you're suffering and you are angry, bitter, and joyless, it means that at some level you've idolized whatever it is you are losing.

The Gospel, however, frees us to revel in our expendability! The Gospel alone provides us with the foundation to maintain radical joy in remarkable loss. Joylessness and bitterness in the crucible of pain happen when we lose something that we've held onto more tightly than God.

# CHAPTER NINETEEN

## Loved By Him In Christ

In the book of John, the Savior Himself lays down this vital principle of growth; **"If you abide in me, and My words abide in you…"(John 15: 7)** His words stir up faith, prayer, hunger, and a desire for God. In the next few verses a crucial part of abiding in the Lord Jesus is emphasized; **"As the Father loved Me, I also have loved you; abide in My love,"(John 15:9).** The command is **"Abide in My love."** He tells us to never forget and always to keep before our hearts this great truth-**His love for us!** This was the secret to Paul's courageous and daring faith, it was rooted in the Savior's love. He declared, **"I live by faith in the Son of God, who loved me and gave Himself for me," (Galatians 2:20).** Believing and receiving His love is the only way to experience His joy abiding in our hearts.

### God is Not Slack

**In 2 Peter, the Scriptures clearly state that with the Lord a day is just like a thousand years, and a thousand years are like a day.** "The Lord is not slow in keeping his promise, as some understand slowness. Instead he is patient with you, not wanting anyone to perish, but everyone to come to repentance. But the day of the Lord will come like a thief the heavens will disappear with a roar; the elements will be destroyed by fire, and the earth and everything done in it will be laid bare.

**No matter what human beings choose to believe, the time bomb threatening all human life, continues to tick. The delicate balance of numerous dangerous factors is so fragile that just a major war could spell doom for man's survival.** "If those days had not been cut short, no one would survive, but for the sake of the elect those days will be shortened. At that time if

*Beauty for Ashes*

anyone says to you, 'Look, here is the Messiah!' or, 'There he is!' Do not believe it. For false messiahs and false prophets will appear and perform great signs and wonders to deceive, if possible, even the elect. See, I have told you ahead of time." **(Matthew 24:22-25)**

So, even though what we want in the world is to be crushing the bad guys and rescuing the victims, what we ***need*** is to the one in need of rescue. When everything's falling apart around us, we want to think that we've got it under control, that we'll find a way to win in the end. But when everything's falling apart around us, we need to remember there's someone in control up there, a safety net, someone to make sure that the ending is the right one.

And as our lives go on, sometimes full of failure and uncertainty, we can find our joy in knowing the real Hero has written a victorious ending to the story, one in which **He gets the credit**, but we indeed get **the rescue**. *Without the shedding of blood there's no remission of sin.*

### New Choices, New freedom

**"Now a slave has no permanent place in the family, but a son belongs to it forever. So if the Son sets you free, you will be free indeed." (John 8:35-36)**

When we are faced with decisions in life, our choices affect our outcome. The decision to believe in Jesus Christ and make Him the Lord of your life is the most important decision you will ever make. This decision affects where your soul will spend eternity – in Heaven with Jesus, or in hell, which was intended for the devil and his fallen angels. Everything in the Old Testament was based on what you earned. Whatever you earned, you passed down to your children, and your children's children. God says in **Exodus 20:6, "But I lavish unfailing love for a thousand generations on those who love me and obey my commands."** Generational blessing and cursing are part of the divine exchange when we are born again. God becomes our Father in Heaven, and we are given the blood of Jesus, the mind of Christ, the spirit of God, and the power to change our very DNA by obeying the Holy Spirit! The enemy will always try to blind you and distort your view of the love of God through tragedy, damaged relationships, broken promises, and disillusionment. God's love is able to reach you this day, and He will pull you out of the deepest pit of your life and set you on the solid rock to stay. The road to overcoming and restoring what is dead began at an old rugged Cross, with Jesus shedding His blood for you and me. ***God gives us Beauty for Ashes!***

No amount of false religion or self-help courses can do in a lifetime what God can do with just one touch of His hand. You cannot restore yourself and overcome age-old generational curses alone. Only the spotless precious blood of Jesus Christ can do it!

Luke recorded this statement Jesus made about an important choice: **"No servant can serve two masters; for either he will hate the one and love the other, or else he will be loyal to one and despise the other," (Luke 16:13).** A superficial faith, not based on Scripture, fails to acknowledge God in moments of need. We must learn to see spiritually by choosing to walk in the Lord's design rather than our own. This walk of trust is what it means to be a Christian. In true faith we must trust God, while in the conventional sight of the mind, we lack such trust and are blind.

As the prophet, Habakkuk, says, we must learn to trust God *regardless* of what happens.

**"Though the fig tree may not blossom, Nor fruit be on the vines; Though the labor of the olive may fail, And the fields yield no Food; Though the flock may be cut off from the fold, And there Be no herd in the stalls-Yet will I rejoice in the LORD, I will joy In the God of my salvation. The LORD God is my strength; He will make my feet like deer's feet, And He will make me Walk on my high hills." (Habakkuk 3:17-19)**

God desires total trust from His children. When we have a divided heart, not wanting to make a sure commitment to follow God, in the Scripture God says; **"I know your deeds, that you are** neither cold nor hot. I wish you were either one or the other! So because you are lukewarm-neither hot or cold- I am about to spit you out of my mouth. You say, I am rich; I have acquired wealth and do not need a thing.' But you do not realize that you are wretched, pitiful, poor, blind and naked. I counsel you to buy from me gold refined in the fire, so you can become rich; and white clothes to wear, so you can cover your shameful nakedness; and salve to put on your eyes, so you can see. Those whom I love a rebuke and discipline. So be earnest and repent. Here I am! I stand and knock. If anyone hears my voice and opens the door, I will come in and eat with that person, and they with me." (Revelation 3:13-20)**

Our whole perspective of life changes when we meet God in His glorious sinlessness when we see Him in His majestic holiness. This change is brought about by repentance of sin, and then by coming to a place of humility and brokenness before the Lord. This humble repentance is essential to a real change in the inner person. The prophet, Isaiah, experienced this metanoia. **"In the year that King Uzziah died I saw also the Lord sitting Upon a throne, high and lifted up, and His train filled The temple...Then I said, Woe is me! For I am undone; Because I am a man of unclean lips: for mine eyes Have seen the King, the LORD of hosts." (Isaiah 6:1-1, KJV)**

In the new perspective of a life recast by repentance, you will see God as He really is and not as you may have imagined Him. Recognition of the Savior and His redemption is your *only hope*. Without repentance all external change is mere pretense. There is no greater chapter in the Bible on repentance than Psalm 51. It represents the cry of a broken, contrite and humbled heart that longs to see and to be close to his Lord and Creator again. This cry of repentance was inspired by the historical background of King David's fall into sin. (See 2 Samuel 11-12.) David understood that his sin had separated him from His God, and that thought broke his heart.

David's conspicuous blindness is apparent blindness in his greed and reckless disregard for human life. It was all so unnecessary. David had all that he needed in his life, but he was unable to see clearly. He had forgotten the God who had done so much for him- the God he had known so well when He wrote Psalm 23. David was blind to his own sin, and his heart was hardened to God's will.

## Spiritual Blindness Exposed

The prophet Nathan came to David after these events and told him a story about a wealthy man who had many sheep but took his poor neighbor's only lamb in order to feed a visiting guest. David's reaction was immediate. He thought that this wealthy man surely deserved death. With his eyes clouded by sin, David could not recognize himself in this story. Nathan admonished, *"Thou art the man!"* Instantly, David's vision was restored in that moment of truth, *and he exclaimed, "I have sinned."*

David had certainly sinned against God. He had rejected and mocked God's commandments. He had been ungrateful for all the good that God had extended to him. In this instance, David had forgotten the goodness God had shown to him, ever since the days he had been a shepherd boy, to be seated upon the throne representing God's rule over His people. David had counted God's wisdom as foolishness and did not heed his commandments. David, the earthly king cast aside God's friendship to please himself. David dragged God's glory into muck in which he had plunged himself. He neither feared nor honored God at that point. For a time, he willfully cast aside all the sweetness of God's beautiful holiness while he embraced his own greedy desires.

Self-redemption is every human being's fondest hope, but it's also our impossible dream. The assertion is simple: we can't redeem ourselves.

Humans refuse to believe that we are beyond helping ourselves. In fact, we often protest that God only helps those who do help themselves. We dearly wish that we could atone for our mistakes of the past, and say, "Thanks but no thanks" to the offered atoning death of another. We're uncomfortable owing someone so much. We only acknowledge our need for a savior when the idol of self-salvation is unceremoniously ripped from our grasp. Until some tragic "event" serves as the hammer of God, finally convincing us and those we love that a savior from within is not enough! Today, let us celebrate the good news that **we have a Redeemer**, and **He is not us.**

## Sincere Repentance

"I acknowledge my transgressions, And my sin is always before me Against You, You only, have I sinned, And done this evil in Your sight." (Psalm 51:3-4)

You cannot cause a man with a full stomach to cry out in the way that a hungry man does. Likewise, you cannot make a man with a good opinion of himself cry out for mercy like one who feels- sees- his vileness. **Psalm 51** shows us that David, with his heart freshly stung and aware, was now humiliated and spiritually crushed. He was overwhelmed with sorrow. In Psalm 51, David is finally open, honest, and transparent with God. David had finished lying to himself and excusing himself- he finally took full responsibility for his actions and then sought God's forgiveness.

David had seen that the evil he had committed in God's sight had defiled others, had wronged them, and had brought them down to his own level. He had at one time esteemed God's lovingkindness as better than life itself. By repenting, David came to see again that his life meant nothing without the warmth of God's smile upon him. His sense from separation from God and his sense of God's displeasure were more painful to him than having his bones broken. Knowing that the dark night of his soul would be banished by finding God's reassuring love once again, David prayed fervently:

> Make me hear joy and gladness,
>
> That the bones you have broken may rejoice,
>
> Hide your face from my sins,

And blot out all my iniquities.    –Psalm 51:8-9

In his past, David had known such joy as the strength of his life, but it had been a long time since his soul could say, as it once had, *"My cup runneth over."* Seeing his sin with his restored vision, he could not continue with his life unless God gave him this joy again. **"Restore to me the joy of your salvation, and uphold me with *thy* free spirit." (Psalm 51:12)**

David's cry, **"Do not take your Holy Spirit from me," (Psalm 51:11**), tells us that David knew he could not live for God without the help of the Holy Spirit. And neither can you and me. In his repentance from dependence of self, he cast himself on the everlasting arms of God. David saw that he needed God's hand upon his soul to keep him from evil. He needed the river of God to flow through his soul again, so that he might find his refreshment in the pleasure of God. When God answered this heartfelt humble prayer, David looked forward to being able to say once more, **"My soul follows close behind You; Your right hand upholds me," (Psalm 63:8).** No sin is too big for the precious spotless blood of Jesus Christ! We've been forgiven, no matter what've done.

David came to see that God could cleanse him and make him **"whiter than snow" (Psalm 51:7).** It became clear that God could remove the sense of defilement and guilt. David sought the relief that only God could give.

You might reasonably ask, "How could David ever believe that he could be forgiven?" You might also observe that when his eyes were finally opened, it would be easy for him to see himself as a hopeless case. Yet, there was one thing that David knew that helped him in his despair. God had promised this king of Israel that He would be a Father to him: **"I will be his Father, and he shall be My son," (2 Samuel 7:14;** see also **Psalm 2:6-7)** What David desired most was to be restored in his relationship with God. God was his Father, his first love, his joy and portion in life. This relationship is what David had cast aside, and it was to this he desired to return.

David would one day understand intimately how a father's heart feels toward a rebellious child. When his proud, self-serving son, Absalom, was killed, David displayed great love and pity crying, **"O my son Absalom-if only I had died in your place!" (2 Samuel 18:33)** To plead God's grace, David knew that he was pleading the grace and mercy in the heart of God *as His Father.*

David could faithfully believe that he would be forgiven, in spite of the greatness of his sin. To know the Father-heart of God is to be saved from desperation and despair, which follows when we harden our hearts, pursue our sin, and are then awakened to see the horror of our ugly, ungodly selves.

"Does Psalm 51 apply to all of us or only those who have fallen as far as David had? You might say, "I'm a good person. I have not committed any act like David did. Am I as bad as David?" Yet the Bible declares that there is none righteous. As it is written **"There is no one righteous, not even one; there is no one who understand; there is no one who seeks God. All have turned away, they have together become worthless there is no one who does good, not even one. Their throats are open graves; their tongues practice deceit. The poison of vipers is on their lips. Their mouths are full of cursing and bitterness. Their feet are swift to shed blood; ruin and misery mark their ways, and the way of peace they do not know. There's no fear of God in their eyes." (Romans 3:10-18)**

And if I think I am righteous, I am profoundly deceived. Isaiah 65:5 describes such a person as one who says to God, **"Keep to yourself, do not come near me, for I am holier than thou."** God replies that such spiritual blindness is "Smoke in my nostrils, a fire that burns all day." God is great, glorious, majestic, almighty and infinitely holy.

It has been said: "If we cannot be awakened to see our danger, we cannot be saved." That is because we will blindly continue in sin **"as an oxen goes to the slaughter" (Proverbs 7:22).** Each of us falls into the category of "the greatest sinner" because we have broken the greatest commandment: **"You shall love the LORD your God with all your heart," (Deuteronomy 6:5).** Before we are born again, we all have put our "self" above God. We have forgotten God and have not lived in thankfulness toward him. We have all rejected God's appointed King over our lives- **King Jesus.**

We could also ask the question, "Am I better than the Apostle Paul?" Paul painted himself as chief among sinners. **(1 Timothy 1:15**) The Scriptures are clear in declaring that all have sinned and come short of the glory of God **(Romans 3:32).** If we take God's Word to heart, we will realize that we can only be reconciled to God by coming in repentant faith to the welcoming arms of Jesus who declared, **"Come to Me...and I will give you rest..."(Mathew 11:28).** To begin living a life that is pleasing to God, we must receive salvation through the blood of Christ alone, who paid for our sin through His death on the Cross. Accepting that foundation based on the Savior's life and death, we will experience a new birth: **"...no other foundation can anyone lay than that which is laid, which is Jesus Christ." (1 Corinthians 3:11)**

To answer the question, "Am I as bad as David in God's sight? We must respond, "Surely I am!" And then, in humble repentance, we can know the wonderful cleansing that David experienced.

A God who knows us can be a scary thing. It's the kind of thing we say we want, but when reality comes into focus, we can get a little scared. A God who knows us can turn out to be something we don't want and something we want to hide from. We are sure we can escape God in the same way that we escape our parents or any of the other oppressive forces in our lives. So, what are we to do with a God who claims to "fill heaven and earth," a God who explicitly says there's nowhere we can hide from Him? Well, we have to hope that there's a disconnect between what we fear will happen when He finds us and what will *actually* happen. The good news is that there *is* such a disconnect, and its cause *is Jesus Christ.*

We fear a holy God because we know that when a holy God finds an unholy us, the only possible reaction is rejection and exile. We read all over the Bible about "the outer darkness" and a God who says "I never knew you" to people who don't live up to

His standard. We sinners need this to not be the last word. And thankfully it isn't.

On account of Jesus Christ and His sacrifice for us, when God finds us hiding from Him in the deepest, darkest corners of our consciousness, He actually says to us, "I love you." He seeks us out, finds us, dies for us, and raises us to new life in Him. Today, remember that although your impulse is to hide, you have been found by God and loved by Him in Christ.

### Self-Doom Leads to Failure

When we begin our walk with the Lord, we genuinely wish to be godly and to avoid sin. This righteous desire puts us in a frame of mind of wanting to keep all of God's ways. Instead, the Gospel is for those who have realized that they can't carry the weight of the world on their shoulders. Only when God drives us to the end of ourselves do we begin to see life in the Gospel. The good news is that Christianity in its original, most authentic expression understands God chiefly as Savior and human beings chiefly as those in need of being saved.

Similarly, seeking to live our life and practice our faith by our own power, determination, diligence, and discipline means relying on self, which dooms us to failure. Rather we must learn to rest upon the omnipotent, tireless arm of God, which can enable us, sustain us, and raise us up. As we learn to wait on God and receive direction from Him, we will do those works He shows us to do and in the way, He shows us to do them. Then we will know true success in living for God. However, when we rely on our own strengths and self-striving, it will result in limited effectiveness and frustrated failures.

"Martha, a friend of Jesus, expressed her frustration loud to the Master. While her sister Mary sat at Jesus' feet in adoration, Martha was left alone to prepare the meal for their guests. Mary cast herself and her eternal destiny upon Jesus and wanted to spend her time in communion with Christ. Martha's faith, like that of so many of us, sort to do God's work through busy-ness and striving rather than through the more effective use of life, resting in Jesus' presence, being **"...strengthened with the might through His Spirit in the inner man." (Ephesians 3:16)**

This insightful episode in Jesus' life does not teach us that preparing a meal is wrong. Rather, it speaks to the priority and emphasis of a life that made natural food more important than spiritual "food"- communing with the Master. The Scriptures record that **"Martha was distracted with much serving," (Luke 10:40)** In the very presence of Jesus, Martha did not enjoy a relationship with Him because of her inordinate concern with her own works. Jesus' loving response to Martha revealed his concern for her: **"Martha, Martha, you are worried and troubled about many things. But one thing is needed, and Mary has chosen that good part, which will not be taken away from her," (Luke 10:41-42).**

While Martha's focus was on herself, and her need for personal control and self-directed activity, she also wanted to serve God her own way and not God's way. Mary's life on the other hand is justified by Jesus and abandoned to Him. Mary did all things through God's rest and worshipped at His feet. Of course, this battle of focusing on self, and our need for personal control, and self-directed activity entraps the best of us believers, in the walls of sin, death, of fear, anxiety, insecurity and self-salvation. The battle points us to another battle that God unconditionally and single-handedly fought for us. Jesus calls us to Himself, like Mary chose to do, we are to do all things through God's rest and to worship Him.

*It is not that we keep His commandments first, and that then He loves; but that He loves us, and then we keep His commandments.-AUGUSTINE*

When I focus on myself and my need to direct my own activities, without being directed by the Word of God or by His Spirit, I am serving only myself. However, in my abandonment to God I can rest in Him. As I choose to become dependent on God, I am dispossessed of anything of significance other than God alone.

After the disobedience of Adam and Eve, mankind has struggled with his independence from God. Though God has continually revealed to mankind His way to return to relationship with Him, people have chosen to follow their own ways.

A heart that is abandoned to God will learn to "see" the ways of God and will do only those things that please Him. In that way we will truly be followers of Jesus, who declared of Himself, **"I must work the works of Him who sent Me while it is day; the night is coming when no one can work," (John 9:4).** Sometimes it takes being in a situation not only to understand Scripture, but to experience it at a different level. **"He made Him who knew no sin to be sin on our behalf that we might become the righteousness of God in Him," (2 Corinthians 5:21).** The truth is, when you behold Jesus more and more and see His love, His forgiveness, His abundant grace, and His gift of righteousness purchased for you with His own blood, you will be transformed supernaturally. What you see or how others see you is not as important as how God sees you. When you see Jesus and receive His love and grace every day, your heart is transformed inwardly.

This is not an outward behavior modification. This is when that fear begins to dissolve in His perfect love, and that condemnation arising from past mistakes is cleansed by His precious blood. When you know you are precious in His sight, and that God has loved you with an everlasting love; then all you can do is to praise Him in advance for His plan for you.

What are His plans for me? He's at work in me and in my situation to break old patterns of thought and action, to create within me both the desire and the power to do His gracious will… and to make me a joy to Him in new ways. In the Scriptures He says that, **"No weapon that is formed against thee shall prosper; and every tongue that shall rise against thee in judgement thou shalt condemn. This is the heritage of the servants of the LORD, and their righteousness is of me, saith the LORD."(Isaiah 54:17)**

**"So shall my word be that goeth forth out of my mouth: it shall not return unto me void, but it shall accomplish that**

**which I please, and it shall prosper *in the thing* whereto I sent it." (Isaiah 55:11)**

Aren't you thankful that God does not hold a pair of scales and asks us to pile up enough good works to outweigh our sins, failures and our unworthiness...that it's all by grace through faith. What an incentive to live a life that pleases Him, a life that brings God joy and not grief!

It is such a joy to know that through Christ I am all right as a person, for in Christ I am righteous with His righteousness. I am justified - just as if I'd never sinned! At this moment and forever: totally clean, every stain removed and forgiven, no matter how great or recent a failure I've had to confess, or how often I have failed. You see, God Himself said this - and His Word cannot be broken -"No condemnation now hangs over the head of those who are in Christ Jesus. The Judge, the Authority, the Chief Justice of the Supreme Court of all the earth has said and it is established.

**"He has not dealt with us according to our sins, Nor rewarded us according to our iniquities. For as high as the heavens are above the earth, so great is His lovingkindness toward those who fear Him. As far as the east is from the west, so far has He removed our transgressions from us. Just as a father has compassion on his children, So the LORD has compassion on those who fear Him."(Psalm 103:10-13)**

Whether we have abundance in our bank accounts, good reliable jobs and everything is fine and dandy, the truth is life puts burdens on us and we become too busy for God, but the LORD is saying to us, you are not the car you drive, the house you live in or the job you have, the truth is that you are created in the image of God. Then God said, **"Let us make mankind in our image, in our likeness, so that they may rule over the fish in the sea and the birds in the sky, over the livestock and all the animals, and over all the creatures that move along the ground." So God created mankind in His own image, in the image of God he created them; male and female he created them. God blessed them and said to them, "Be fruitful and increase in number; fill the earth and subdue it. Rule over the fish in the sea and** the birds of the sky and over every living creature that moves on the ground."(Genesis 1:26-28)

Marvelous are God's works! I thank Him that He uniquely designed and created me with the same precision He used in creating the universe, He formed me in love exactly to His specifications. God embroidered me with great skill in my mother's womb.

I'm grateful that my looks, my abilities, and my personality are like a special picture frame in which God can portray His grace and beauty, His love, His strength, His faithfulness, to the praise of His glory. And therefore, I can thank God that He has gifted me for the special purposes He has in mind for my life. And so, I thank God for His wisdom. And for allowing the things that have influenced me throughout my life-the things that have prepared my heart to respond to Him and to live for His glory. I might not have turned to God if things had been different.

**"For Thou didst form my inward parts; Thou didst weave me in my mother's womb. I will give thanks to Thee, for I am fearfully and wonderfully made; Wonderful are Thy works, and my soul knows it very well,"(Psalm 139:13-14)**. It's wonderful to know that God is not in the least dissatisfied with your inborn talents, intelligence, aptitudes, appearance, and personality, for His hands have made and fashioned you. You are one of God's original masterpieces!

You are not your own, you've been bought with a price, all the silver and gold in this world could never purchase you. You've been bought by the precious blood of Jesus Christ. You belong to God. **"You have persevered and have endured hardship for my name, and have not grown weary. Yet I hold this against you: You have forsaken the love you had first. Consider how far you have fallen! Repent and do the things you did at first…" (Revelation 2:3-5)**

In spite of all that God has provided, including the Holy Spirit's presence and power, we don't automatically praise and give thanks. So why do I ever get so busy, even in my quiet time, that I bypass the delightful opportunity to extol and adore my wonderful Lord? And why do I at times feel reluctant to praise in the midst of everyday trials?

Satan's major strategies is to divert us from praise, after all, he knows that God delights in our praise, and that doesn't exactly make him happy. Even as believers our flesh will also prevail over our spirits, dampening our desire to glorify God. With our focus on God's love for us, praise and worship for all he has done for us through Christ our Savior, The Lord our God will fill every part with praise, that our whole being may proclaim, Thy being and Thy ways. Not for the lip of praise alone, but that God will tune my heart to sing Thy grace and streams of mercy never ceasing in praise.

In our journey, we get weary, but the Word reminds us to focus on the Maker of Heaven and Earth and remember that everything we need has been provided for in Christ...seeking first the Kingdom of God and His righteousness and all these things shall be added unto us.

The mind always wants to doubt the sincerity or sufficiency of our confession. Confession is not blaming, pointing a finger at others without pointing a finger at yourself, confession is so much more, and it is a radical reliance on grace. This is a profanation of our trust in God's goodness. "What I did was wrong," we admit responsibly, "but your grace Oh Lord is so much greater than my sin, so I confess it." Like the prodigal son cried saying; **"Father, I have sinned against heaven and before you, and I am no longer worthy to be called your son," (Luke 15:18-19).** And remember the tax collector; **"But the tax collector stood at a distance. He would not even look up to heaven, but beat his breast and said, 'God, have mercy on me, a sinner,' (Luke 18:13).** Like David we need a prayer of grace-based confession.

Oh, how we forget that we've been Boazed and bought, foot washed and indwelled by Christ. We can risk honesty with God. The moment we choose to go to Him as we would a trusted friend, and explain the pain and revisit the transgression together, welcoming the Holy Spirit's probing and healing touch, trusting

*Beauty for Ashes*

His ability to receive our confession more than our ability to make it.

However daunting and distressing your battle with sin may be, you can find some encouragement in Paul's discussion. At least Paul knew there was a battle in his soul. To be engaged in this battle at all shows you have been born again and do not desire to sin. The unbeliever delights in his sin or simply rationalizes it when it is convenient. Paul felt disappointed in his sin and longed for God's help to grow. This attitude toward sin is the beginning of spiritual sight!

We also may ask why Paul, as a mature believer, still could speak of this battle with sin in the present tense: *"I am doing"*; but *"I hate it."* The answer lies in the realization that we are never completely free from sin and that the closer we get to God the more sensitive we become to what displeases Him. If we have tender hearts toward God, we will always be ashamed of our sins, which are fundamentally based in **"the lust of the flesh, the lust of the eyes, and the pride of life" (1 John 2:16).** These are temptations and failures that is our human lot, as long as we remain in this world.

It is true, if we are vigilant, that we are sometimes stronger than the temptation we face and gain a victory over it. However, at times we simply do not resist the devil, the flesh, and the world in the moment of temptation. As believers, we will finally come to our senses and cry out in despair within ourselves, as Paul did, to receive the divine deliverance offered us.

The believer in Jesus does not ultimately despair; he thanks God, as Paul did, for the victory he has in Jesus his Savior. **(Romans 7:25)** He learns to go again to the cleansing blood of Christ and receive forgiveness, with no condemnation **(See Romans 8:1).** Instead of despair, he rejoices that once again his faith in the power of Christ's redemption has rescued him again, and he thanks God for not abandoning him in his sin. He is assured that one day this battle against sin will be over. Until then, he has found the pathway to progressing toward full faith. The Law may expose bad behavior, but only grace can win the heart.

Most importantly I am in agreement with God's word in (Luke 4:18-19). God cares for you and me, he has not left us as orphans. The Bible says that all things work together for good for those who love God and choose to put themselves in alignment with His purposes. You can choose to be happy and experience the emotional blessing of supernatural joy, even in an undesirable circumstance, because you're drawing joy from the belief that God is always at work and He will create something good for you.

Trespass might increase. But for Christians? The Law works absolutely. "Therefore no one will be declared righteous in God's sight by the works of the law; rather, through the law we become conscious of our sin" (Romans 3:20). Thank God Christ has come for failures.

God is no respecter of persons. What He did for me, He will do for you. God is able to restore you in every place or area that you have been violated, hurt, offended, wounded or disappointed. **"Be strong and take heart, all you who hope in the LORD." (Psalm 31:24)**

God has enabled me to grow from a place of victim to a place of victory. When Jesus went to be with His Father, He sent the Holy Spirit to be with us, and to give us all the good gifts we could never earn on our own. When God looks at us, His gaze finds what His voice has declared! We have been given gifts by the Holy Spirit. And the real miracle is, it actually happens! We have faith where none existed before. We are given wisdom in a difficult situation. We understand God's will in a situation without even knowing how we do so. Each one of these things is a miracle, because they come directly from God. They are *His* gifts, freely given to us.

This Spiritual sight of God's forgiveness for my sins, has through the power of the Holy Spirit helped me to live the life that God has for me. To confess Christ as Lord and Savior, is to become a new creation in Christ Jesus. The "old things" have passed away and all things "have become new", is only possible in Christ Jesus. I have been redeemed from the curse of the Law because of the precious blood of Jesus. The way to be delivered from self is to be occupied by Christ. We are forgiven by the quality of God's grace, never by the quantity of our work or goodness.

Identify the source of your worries. Did you grow up in a fear-filled family, always feeling insecure, never measuring up, and never hearing words of affirmation and approval? Are you listening to messages of doom, hearing only about what's wrong, and how much worse it's going to get? What's the source of your anxiety; what feeds your worries? Until you express your fears you can't expel them.

Putting your fear into words disrobes them. They look weak and silly standing there naked. You must fight hard to express your fear. You must fight hard to shine the light of words upon it. Because if you don't, if your fear becomes a wordless darkness that you avoid, perhaps even manage to forget, you open yourself to further attacks of fear because you never truly fought the opponent who defeated you. Am not saying that you should announce your fears, but I am encouraging you to trust God with your most intimate fears, expose each and every one of them as the Holy Spirit leads you. Let your problems drive you into the arms of Jesus Christ.

It is good news that God doesn't reward the good and punish the bad. If He did, that would be bad news for all of us. Our God comes to the bad people, giving them His Son's righteousness in exchange for their sins. *He gives us beauty for ashes!*

If you make Him your hiding place, the LORD will protect you from trouble and surround you with songs of deliverance. Though many are the woes of the wicked, but the LORD's unfailing love surrounds the one who trusts in him. God will instruct you and teach you in the way you should go; He will counsel you with His loving eye on you. You have a place in God's Kingdom that is eternal, and nothing can separate you and me from His limitless, intensely personal love. The one love that is not the least bit based on how much you and I deserve it, the one love that can never lessen or fail! **"See how great a love the**

**Father has bestowed upon us, that we should be called children of God; and such we are..." (1 John 3:1)**